"But Will It Work with *Real* Students?"

Contributing Authors of Narratives and Teacher Responses

Cindy L. Aubuchon, McCutcheon High School, Lafayette, Indiana

Sheila A. Bailey, West Junior High School, Columbia, Missouri

Kevin Basmadjian, Michigan State University, East Lansing, Michigan

Lynore M. Carnuccio, ESL Education Consultant, Yukon, Oklahoma

Deborah Dean, Brigham Young University, Provo, Utah

Stephen L. Fisher, Wausau West High School, Wausau, Wisconsin

Kerry A. Hoffman, Indiana University–Purdue University, Indianapolis, Indiana

Carla Gubitz Jankowski, Morton East High School, Cicero, Illinois

Kevin B. Kienholz, Emporia State University, Emporia, Kansas

Sharon M. Lauderman, Donegal High School, Mount Joy, Pennsylvania

Terry Martin, Central Washington University, Ellensburg, Washington

Jeanne Muzzillo, Purdue University, West Lafayette, Indiana

Judith B. O'Loughlin, Ho-Ho-Kus Public School, Ho-Ho-Kus, New Jersey

M. Michele Pittard, Wabash College, Crawfordsville, Indiana

Natalie Scavone, Cayuga-Onondaga BOCES, Syracuse, New York

Lisa Schade, Purdue University, West Lafayette, Indiana

Joy A. Seybold, Indiana Professional Standards Board and Indiana State Teachers Association, Indianapolis, Indiana

Lucy Stanovick, Oakland Junior High School, Columbia, Missouri

Laura Whitcombe, McCutcheon High School, Lafayette, Indiana

Marguerite Wollerton, Faith Academy, Manila, Philippines

"But Will It Work with *Real* Students?"

Scenarios for Teaching Secondary English Language Arts

Janet Alsup
Purdue University

Jonathan Bush
Western Michigan University

National Council of Teachers of English
1111 W. Kenyon Road, Urbana, Illinois 61801-1096

Staff Editor: Bonny Graham

Interior Design: Doug Burnett

Cover Design: Pat Mayer

NCTE Stock Number: 03898-3050

It is the policy of NCTE in its journals and other publications to provide a fo-
rum for the open discussion of ideas concerning the content and the teaching
of English and the language arts. Publicity accorded to any particular point of
view does not imply endorsement by the Executive Committee, the Board of
Directors, or the membership at large, except in announcements of policy,
where such endorsement is clearly specified.

Library of Congress Cataloging-in-Publication Data

Alsup, Janet.
    But will it work with real students? : scenarios for teaching secondary
English language arts / Janet Alsup, Jonathan Bush.
        p. cm.
Includes bibliographical references and index.
    ISBN 0-8141-0389-8 (pbk.)
    1. Language arts (Secondary)—United States. 2. English teachers—
Training of—United States. I. Bush, Jonathan. II. Title.
    LB1631.A47 2003
    428' .0071'273—dc22

                                                                    2003017860

Contents

Acknowledgments

Janet Alsup would like to thank all of the teacher-authors who contributed to this text. Without their willingness to narrate classroom experiences and share pedagogical expertise, this book could not have been written. Thanks also go to the Department of English at Purdue University for providing support for research and writing, to the NCTE reviewers who supplied much useful feedback, and to Professor Roy F. Fox of the University of Missouri for his excellent mentorship. Last, she is grateful to all of her former students, both secondary and postsecondary, for facilitating her growth as a teacher over the years.

Jonathan Bush gives thanks to Erin, Delaney, Avery, and Owen, who help him keep things in perspective. Also, thanks go to his colleagues at Western Michigan University for their support. Finally, thanks to Zarina Hock at NCTE for her unfailing support and expert advice throughout the project.

Introduction: Situations and Scenarios—Narratives from the Secondary English Class

But will it work with *real* students?" Many preservice and practicing teachers find themselves asking this question when they go to a teachers' conference or read about the latest innovative teaching method in a professional book or journal. Strategies presented at conferences, in university methods courses, or at inservice workshops sound exciting and seem to have great classroom potential. There is little doubt that most of these ideas are theoretically sound and can inspire teachers to modify and improve lessons or even entire curricula. Implementing these strategies or approaches in actual secondary school classrooms, however, can be difficult. Too often the reality simply does not match the expectation. Such disappointments are demoralizing; they can cause teachers to be wary of new approaches and even create cynicism toward teacher education conferences, classes, and pedagogical books.

This is where our book comes in. Our primary goal in writing *"But Will It Work with* Real *Students?"* was to bridge the gap between the "good ideas" and classroom practice, between idealistic plans and day-to-day classroom life. Many times teachers learn new approaches in classes or workshops but never have the opportunity to discuss the results after they implement them. If the experimental activity doesn't work, teachers might not have the time or the resources to figure out how to make it work better next time. Therefore, the activity or approach is scrapped. But discussion and critical reflection are essential to the professional development of the teacher, especially the new teacher. Instead of handing out ideas like candy and then disappearing, teacher educators must discover ways to provide support for teachers both during their initial education and after they leave our university classes and begin to teach. We hope this book can provide such support for the secondary English teacher through narratives about classroom practices and thoughtful critical responses to them. Along with discussions of related research and theory, the chapters can be prompts for discussion and critical reflection about both familiar and innovative classroom practices.

Past or present high school and middle school teachers wrote all of the narratives and responses in this book. In the narratives, they share both classroom successes and failures—stories of teaching executed "by the book" but lacking textbook results and stories of teaching that resulted in successful (and even joyful) student learning. We present these stories to prompt discussion about issues central to English teaching in secondary schools, and to help us reach this goal we follow the stories with one or two thoughtful, reflective responses written by other English teachers and teacher educators. These responses offer praise and constructive criticism and are not meant to be definitive answers to the issues or problems presented; instead, they are intended to further professional dialogue and prompt readers to think more deeply about each narrative and the issues it presents. Additionally, each chapter summarizes current theory and research relevant to the issue or pedagogical concept being discussed and highlights both "best practices" and major controversies in the teaching of that particular aspect of secondary English language arts.

We borrow the phrase "best practice" from Zemelman, Daniels, and Hyde's *Best Practice: New Standards for Teaching and Learning in America's Schools* (1998). In later chapters, we cite many of their characteristics defining effective literacy teaching, and when Zemelman et al. do not address a particular pedagogical issue, we borrow their organizational schemata for best practices to create our own list of applicable characteristics for effective teaching.

We chose to structure this book around narratives, for narrative as a way of learning has a long history. Anthropologists, psychologists, historians, and folklorists have been using narrative as a way to study human behavior for decades. Every culture has its own body of myth and legend to help explain the world and its mysteries. Many academic disciplines center on narrative as the basis for knowledge, including history, literary studies, and even, to some extent, psychology and philosophy. In short, learning about and by human beings seems to be inherently connected to narrative. As we write this introduction, we can easily brainstorm a list of a few of the many historical and contemporary uses of narrative in human learning, whether that learning be personal or professional/academic:

- To discover identity or find one's voice
- To solve professional problems through analysis of "cases"

- To come to terms with personal trauma
- To teach lessons or share "morals" about human life
- To represent our world and ourselves to those who may come after us

Of course, there are many more uses of narrative that we have not listed. The point is that story is a natural part of human life. We tell stories at the dinner table, at lunch, to our friends, and about our friends. Most of our talk almost naturally occurs as narrative, not as exposition, persuasion, or description. Research has been conducted in composition studies demonstrating that narrative writing is the first and most easily facilitated type of adolescent writing (Moffett, 1983). When our students engage in other "modes" while writing or speaking, they are often doing so in the service of telling a story.

Veteran teachers report that the best way to learn to teach is by applying what has been previously learned in the classroom to the teaching task at hand. Toward this end, teachers often tell anecdotes about their teaching experiences in the staff room, at after-school get-togethers, and even at conferences focusing on story and narration as ways of learning. Kathy Carter (1993) writes that in recent years story has become an accepted way for teachers to talk and learn about teaching. Educators have moved away from purely quantitative data to describe their experiences. According to Carter, "The core knowledge teachers have of teaching comes from their practice, i.e., from taking action as teachers in classrooms. Teachers' knowledge is, in other words, event structured, and stories, therefore, would seem to provide special access to that knowledge" (p. 7).

In this book, we use stories for the second purpose previously listed: to solve professional problems through analysis of "cases" and subsequent reflection and discussion of these stories with colleagues and mentors. While we do not deny that other benefits from using narrative as a way of learning may result (for example, teachers writing and responding to narratives in this book may be working through classroom "traumas" or attempting to leave a record of their teaching practice for those practitioners who will follow them), we use stories written by teachers in order to explore pedagogical issues central to the middle and high school English teacher. We hope these narratives prompt critical thinking about teaching practices in the language arts classroom.

The following chapters are organized by curricular categories in English language arts, and within each chapter we have included questions for further discussion and suggested learning activities. We have also included annotated bibliographies of related texts for further exploration since one of the key aspects of narrative learning is that stories should be a springboard for reflective practice and teacher growth, useful not only for the practices they explore but also for the larger issues that frame and define them. We return to this notion in depth in the last chapter when we describe the practice of "narrative action research" as conducted by teachers in an effort to improve their practice through heightened critical reflection.

We realize that the following chapters in no way cover every possible area of interest or concern to the teacher of English in grades 5 through 12, but in the spirit of having to make strategic choices, we decided on seven pedagogical areas that seemed especially interesting and relevant to our contributing authors: literature and reading, writing, language and grammar, second language learning, management and discipline, technology, and standardized testing. Since we cover so much ground, *"But Will It Work with* Real *Students?"* is not a comprehensive look at all of these issues; however, we believe it can be the beginning of an ongoing professional conversation about the teaching of English in the middle and high school. We invite you to turn the page, read the first story, and reflect on your past, present, and future teaching.

1 Narratives about Teaching Literature and Reading

Many of us became English teachers because we were readers. We had that special moment as young adolescents when we were lost in a book, that "flow" moment that Donelson and Nilsen (1997) claim is essential to the creation of a reader. After that moment when the minutes and hours clicked by without notice as "our nose was buried in a book," we have been hooked. When we went to college and declared ourselves English majors, we indulged our passion even more. We took classes in Shakespeare, Faulkner, Chaucer, Milton, and the like. We did not always love these classes (sometimes our professors made them hard to love), but we did learn how literary analysis can deepen our appreciation of a work and can even be fun. Some of us also became literary snobs. We decided that the reading and subsequent analysis of classic texts was essential to literacy.

What many of us forgot between our secondary schooling and the end of our college careers is that not everyone shares our unabashed love of literature. Instead, just the opposite is likely to be true in our classes: many students will profess to hate it. They will not read the texts we assign or will read them only under duress—for example, under the threat of a pop quiz. We, however, want our students to experience the thrill of reading because we know how it affected us, and we believe in the power of books to provide both windows and mirrors into the lives of others and ourselves. Literature as a window allows readers to experience other people, places, and events unfamiliar to them—the quintessential vicarious experience. Literature as a mirror allows readers to see themselves reflected in ways that increase self-awareness and enrich interactions with others. But how do we help our students experience literature as windows and mirrors if they will not—or cannot—read and comprehend the texts we assign?

This brings us to the issues raised in this chapter through narratives about teaching literature and teaching reading. First, what is the difference between literature and reading? The answer to that question is largely based on who is using the terms and for what reason, but generally, *literature* refers to the text that is read and *reading* refers to how successfully an individual interacts with or understands that text. While postmodern understandings of reading address the social and cultural implications of literacy that go beyond the mere decoding of words, the most basic definition of reading is translating and understanding texts at the micro level, while analysis and criticism of texts takes the process to the macro level. Of course, as Louise Rosenblatt (1978) has taught us, one needs both reader and text to make the *poem,* her word for the meaning that results when an active reader encounters a text. The narratives in this chapter tell teachers' stories of teaching reading and literature to secondary school students in a variety of contexts and with a variety of goals, approaches, and results.

What Is *Good* Literature and Reading Instruction?

As you read the narratives in this chapter and the accompanying responses, try to fit the ideas and concepts found in them into your growing philosophy of teaching literature and reading. You may agree with some of the responses offered by experienced teachers, and you may disagree with others. But whether you agree or disagree, the important question is how will you decide which concepts or approaches to incorporate into your own belief system. It is important to have a core set of beliefs or a core philosophical perspective that includes ideas about both theory and practice. Such a philosophical perspective is the foundation upon which a personal pedagogy is built. Our beliefs about literature teaching, for example, privilege the reciprocal relationship of response and analysis. Students should be encouraged to engage with a text to the point that they can offer responses to it, and these responses can be personal, textual, and, finally, analytical and critical—i.e., connected to social, cultural, and even political theories and realities. Allen Carey-Webb (2001), for example, argues for the combination of response-based and cultural studies–based literature teaching to create a curricular and philosophical approach that values individual student response but also links or connects such response to sociocultural meanings and social action.

One of the questions you should consider as you begin to think about your philosophy of teaching literature is *why* you think literature should be taught. Over the years that we have taught methods courses in the teaching of literature, we have asked our students this question. Some students say that literature teaching is important because reading a common body of literature (or a canon) is essential to cultural literacy or making sure human beings share knowledge about a discrete number of texts; others say that teaching literature is important for the vicarious experiences it provides and how it helps us empathize with others. Still other students state that they believe the teaching of literature is important because its close study can teach certain analytical skills. It would not be outside the realm of possibility to say that teachers might teach literature for a combination of all of these reasons. We believe, however, that a teacher should have a philosophical base from which to act, a core set of beliefs that she or he enacts when planning lessons or choosing texts for classroom use. A philosophical approach and pedagogical choices work reciprocally. Your philosophy guides your pedagogy, and pedagogy can modify belief. As you consider this "why" question, consider the following list of approaches that we see as examples of "best practices" in teaching literature. If you want to read more about any of these approaches, consult the annotated bibliography at the end of this chapter.

Characteristics of Effective Secondary Literature and Reading Pedagogy

1. Literature Circles. Literature circles have been around for a long time under a variety of different names and with subtle differences. In the 1980s, we heard them called "literature study groups" and "literature set groups" in addition to the current term, *literature circles*. This term was coined by Harvey Daniels in *Literature Circles: Voice and Choice in the Student-Centered Classroom* (1994*)* and elaborated on by him in *Literature Circles: Voice and Choice in Book Clubs and Reading Groups* (2002). The approach is based on the belief that students must have some choice over what they read and how they read it. In literature circles, each small group of students reads a different book, and often all of the books are thematically linked. Small groups make decisions about how many pages they read per night, how they approach literary discussions, and how they choose to respond to the book as a whole (i.e., a creative project). In Daniels's approach, students are given different roles to play in the group, such as discussion leader, passage master, word wizard, and so forth.

2. Reading Workshops. Reading workshop is a curricular approach to reading instruction that is most often associated with Nancie Atwell (1998). In her book *In the Middle: New Understandings about Writing, Reading, and Learning,* now in its second edition, Atwell describes both writing and reading workshop approaches to teaching middle school language arts. The reading workshop allows students to select their own books in keeping with a general set of guidelines created by the teacher. The students read their own books at their own pace, but they are required to read a certain number of books or pages by the end of a semester or a year. Sometimes students are asked to read in a number of different genres. Additionally, students are required to write journal responses and communicate with their teacher or peers about their reading progress: what they are reading, what they make of it, what they plan to read next, etc. In Atwell's terms, reading workshop provides and encourages "time, ownership, and response" for students as they engage with books.

3. Modeling of Reading and Comprehension Processes. The concept of metacognition is important here. *Metacognition* literally means "thinking about thinking," and metalanguage involves engaging in language or discourse about thinking processes. Being metacognitive means that you are aware of how you read, write, think, or solve problems. While you might not be aware of every step or stage in a complex or elaborate thinking process, successful thinkers and users of language are aware, at least in a general way, of how they go about reading a text and comprehending it or writing a text that explores ideas and issues or makes an argument. Many theorists have suggested that students improve as readers, writers, and thinkers when they become more meta-aware and are able to articulate this awareness to themselves and others (Moffett, 1983; Anderson & Rubano, 1991). Additionally, sometimes students have difficulty reading and writing because they do not understand what a successful process is. Many teachers are so adept at reading and writing, and have been doing it so successfully for so long, that they cannot easily articulate the process to their students. But if teachers do articulate it, they can model the reading/writing process so that students can (1) see that a process exists and (2) observe certain cognitive maneuvers that occur when a successful reader or writer engages with language. Here are some examples of how this modeling can occur in the classroom:

> *"Thinking Aloud" during Reading.* In this activity, the teacher (or a volunteer student) reads something, usually out loud, "on the spot" that he did not have time to examine in advance. As the teacher reads, he talks about what is going on in his head or what he is thinking during the reading experience. While the spoken words can never exactly duplicate the mental processes, they can give a sense that there

is a process that can be messy, recursive, and full of questioning, predicting, and backtracking. Through such an activity, students can see that even skilled readers (like their teacher) do not immediately understand or appreciate the many nuances of a work of literature. (To read more about this process, see Anderson & Rubano [1991].)

Reading Surveys. Teachers can ask students to fill out reading surveys in which they document their history with reading, how many books they read in a given amount of time, when they began reading, what the easiest/hardest part of reading is for them, etc. In this way, the teacher sends the message that becoming a successful reader is not something that happens overnight; on the contrary, it is a lifelong process, and even good readers sometimes do things such as skip words they do not know, read the endings of books first, and stop reading books they do not like. Nancie Atwell (1998) includes sample reading surveys in the appendix of *In the Middle.*

"Before, During, and After" Reading Exercise. This exercise can help students become more aware of their reading processes because it requires them to reflect in writing (and sometimes orally) on a text before, in the middle of, and after reading it. In this way, student readers *predict* what a piece will be about (based on a title, for example, or a book's cover), they stop midstream at least once and *reflect* on the text and make more predictions about what will happen next, and then at the end they look back and *evaluate* their predictions and reflections and *explain* their final reactions. The point is not to try to be right in early predictions, but to give students practice in predicting, questioning, reflecting, and inferring, cognitive activities in which good readers engage.

One way teachers can learn more about the reading behaviors of their students and identify reading strategies to assist them is by conducting a "miscue analysis" with struggling readers. A miscue is an error in reading, and during a miscue analysis a student reads aloud while the teacher marks errors using a special coding system. The pattern of these miscues enlightens the teacher about various strategies the student uses when reading as well as when her reading process breaks down—that is, when meaning is not made of the text. Then the teacher can suggest strategies the student can use to become a better reader (e.g., asking questions, relating texts to background knowledge, comparing difficult words to others she knows, visualizing, predicting, etc.). It's important to realize that making a miscue is not necessarily bad; all readers miscue. As long as appropriate meaning and understanding result, miscuing at worst is irrelevant and at best can be evidence of a strong reader whose eyes are always jumping a few words ahead or who sometimes sacrifices sentence-level accuracy for speed and coherence.

4. Integration of Multiple Types of Texts into the Classroom, Including Electronic and Visual Texts. This characteristic focuses on the idea of "multiple literacies" or the need for modern students to be capable readers of the many types of texts that exist in our modern world: Web sites, advertisements, photographs, films, television shows, and, yes, even books. Educators and researchers such as Carmen Luke (1997), Donna Alvermann, Jennifer Moon, and Margaret Hagood (1999), and Roy Fox (1994) have argued that electronic media, advertisements, television shows, movies, and other visual texts have become important cultural symbols and conveyors of information, and therefore adolescents should learn to critically "read" them if they are to be truly literate. Therefore, the fields of media literacy and cultural studies have introduced a new body of texts into the literature classroom that teachers cannot ignore. The National Council of Teachers of English (NCTE) and the International Reading Association (IRA) (1996) have added to their standards for the teaching of English language arts in the secondary school the ability to interpret and create visual images, and this visual or media literacy is noted side by side with more traditional, print literacies.

Specifics about how to integrate visual and media literacy into your literature curriculum are outside the scope of this book; any discussion of literature teaching would be negligent, however, if it didn't mention multiple texts available for classroom use. Many of the approaches and theories advocated in this book are applicable to the teaching and study of visual texts as well as print ones.

5. Use of Diverse Texts. It is important that teachers make an effort to include literature written by and about diverse people. In other words, when devising a literature curriculum or choosing books to use in a classroom, a teacher should select from a variety of authors in order to include male and female, black and white, and representatives of various ethnic and minority groups. The danger in this selection is the possibility that tokenism will result, or the curriculum will be reconfigured to include certain designated days or weeks during which a variety of races, ethnicities, cultures, or genders are given "air time," yet they remain essentially unintegrated into the literature curriculum at other times of the year. Gonzalez (1990) explains the problems of tokenism versus true multiculturalism:

> Token representation of the histories and literatures of culturally different children are inadequate attempts at engaging and inspiring students' participation in the educational process. One piece of literature or one chapter in American history cannot counter the negative social perceptions that children of minority subcultures have of themselves or that society has of them. A significant proportion of the curriculum must be dedicated to positive ethnic histories and literature and the many contributions that all groups have made to American life. (pp.18–19)

We agree and support Gonzalez's passionate recommendation.

Controversies in Literature and Reading Instruction

As you continue to develop your philosophy of teaching literature and reading, it is helpful to be aware not only of some best practices in literature/reading pedagogy but also of some of the major controversies and arguments in the field concerning literacy teaching and learning in secondary schools. The following are not all of the controversies within the discipline, but they are some of the most prevalent in the field of secondary literature and reading education, and as a teacher of English language arts, you should be familiar with them and with the arguments associated with them.

1. **Young Adult Literature versus Classic Literature.** Many of our students over the years have embraced young adult literature as a genre worthy of study and inclusion in secondary classrooms; others have rejected it as an oversimplified and anti-intellectual literary form. We believe in the value of young adult literature in the classroom (and as a literary genre), but we do not reject the value of classic texts either. We think both can be used successfully in the secondary classroom, sometimes in tandem. Several modern pedagogical theorists, such as Sarah K. Herz and Donald Gallo (1996), Joan F. Kaywell (1993), and Virginia Monseau (1996), have advocated the use of YA and classic books in tandem, suggesting that teachers pair texts with similar themes, thus using one (usually the YA) to facilitate the teaching of the other (normally the classic). In *From Hinton to Hamlet: Building Bridges between Young Adult Literature and the Classics* (1996), Herz and Gallo explain how thematically connecting a young adult and a classic text can help students

become more interested, motivated, and successful in reading and interpreting literature. A teacher could, for example, teach *Great Expectations* by Dickens after teaching Avi's *The True Confessions of Charlotte Doyle*. Both books have young characters (Pip and Charlotte) who are discovering the realities of a hierarchical, class-based society. Both characters end up rejecting the "upper-class" yet superficial individuals in their lives in favor of the sincere, down-to-earth, yet "lower-class," individuals who respect and care for them. By reading the Avi novel first, students can be introduced to these themes (e.g., classism, sexism, identity, and growing up) through a novel that is more structurally and linguistically accessible to them before moving on to the classic novel that is older, unfamiliar in vocabulary and setting, and less likely to capture their immediate attention. While both novels have sophisticated, well-developed themes, together they provide students the opportunity to read contemporary as well as classic literature through theoretical lenses and to engage in intertextual comparisons. Kaywell (1993) has edited four volumes all titled *Adolescent Literature as a Complement to the Classics*, and like Herz and Gallo she offers many examples of thematic linkages between young adult and classic texts and reasons for these connections. Kaywell's books offer practical ideas for connecting dozens of classic texts to diverse YA texts, such as linking *The Grapes of Wrath* by John Steinbeck to *Hatchet* by Gary Paulsen, and *Their Eyes Were Watching God* by Zora Neale Hurston to *Roll of Thunder, Hear My Cry* by Mildred Taylor.

So what is the difference between a young adult and a classic text? The standard definitions are that YA literature is literature written and published specifically with a young adult or adolescent audience in mind, while classic literature was originally written for adults and has stood the test of time, being read and taught in schools for a number of years. Classic literature is often additionally defined as literature that explores and offers new insights into universal human themes or archetypes. Of course, these definitions are fluid. It is not always clear, for example, if a book was written with an adolescent audience in mind, especially since the publishing market has only identified certain types of books as "teen" books since the late 1960s, and sometimes YA books explore universal themes and archetypes as deeply and richly as the quintessential "classic" texts.

Those who wish to learn more about contemporary, quality young adult literature should make themselves familiar with the list of Newbery Medal winners and honor books that can be accessed through the American Library Association's Web site at www.ala.org/.

2. Phonics versus Whole Language Approaches. The terms *phonics* and *whole language* might be more commonly associated with elementary school reading instruction, but the ramifications of the conflict between these approaches are also felt in secondary schools. The easiest way to understand these two camps is to think of pure phonics instruction as moving students from "parts to wholes" and pure whole language instruction as moving students from "wholes to parts." Let us explain. In reading and literacy studies, parts are things like sounds, syllables, and fragments of words, sentences, and texts, and in "pure" phonics instruction teachers begin by teaching students about these parts, believing that once the parts are learned, the whole text will be understood. So students learn sounds, do worksheets about these sounds, and break up sentences and words into their parts or syllables for close study and imitation. Then students move on to reading complete books or whole texts. The "pure" whole language approach is the opposite: it advocates giving students lots of books, reading to them and with them, immersing them in print and language, and believing that as a result of the immersion students will learn the requisite parts through the whole, and probably learn them better and be more interested in reading and more positive about literacy activities. Many reading specialists advocate a combination approach that teaches some phonics within a whole language–based program. This controversy is important to the secondary classroom because some of this "parts to whole" or "whole to parts" debate is evident when teachers, for example, teach lists of spelling words for students to memorize instead of having them identify difficult words from their own reading or writing or ask students to sound out words they don't know instead of relying on context to figure out the meaning of unknown words.

3. Reader Response versus Close Textual Readings. The effective and evenhanded literature teacher can negotiate this controversy, which is similar to the phonics versus whole language debate. Reader-response theory is defined as a transactional approach to understanding a text: the reader interacts with a text and thus "meaning" results. The text in and of itself, without a reader, contains no inherent meaning. Those who advocate close textual readings do not necessarily deny that the reader plays a part in the process; they see reader-response approaches to instruction, however, as pedagogical strategies that put more weight on students' opinions about texts than on the text itself and therefore undermine the efficacy of the text and the intentions of the author.

Close readings of texts often happen in college classrooms. Students are asked to explicate a poem or a prose passage by looking closely at the sentences, the word choices, the images, the figurative language, the symbols or allusions, and other literary devices that are present and then, using a process of deductive analysis, to discover the "meaning" of the text from these semantic and syntactic cues. Response theory happens in classrooms when students are asked to respond personally to a text (e.g., has anything like this ever happened to you? or Do you like this book and why/why not?) and then move from these responses to a more analytical or critical reading. Personal response is seen as essential to such higher-order thinking.

While these processes can be seen as mutually exclusive, we do not think they are. Is it not possible for a teacher to ask students to engage in close readings sometimes and other times ask them to respond personally or individually to a text? Why not encourage students to engage in both of these activities during the reading of a single text? Louise Rosenblatt argues in *Literature as Exploration* (1983) and Ben F. Nelms argues in *Literature in the Classroom: Readers, Texts, and Contexts* (1988) that a movement occurs in literary analysis from reading, through response, to analysis, and finally to social/cultural criticism. In their view, and in ours, both reader response and close analysis are essential to a truly critical reading experience, and they happen in a cognitive and emotional/psychological sequence.

Louise Rosenblatt is credited with applying reader-response theory to the secondary classroom, through her description of transactional theory. Her first text, *Literature as Exploration* (1938/1983), emphasizes the process of reading as a way for students to use past experiences to respond to literature while also building new understandings of their culture and increased empathy for others. Rosenblatt's second book, *The Reader, the Text, the Poem* (1978), develops her idea of a transactional understanding of reading. She believes that meaning is created through an interaction between a reader and a text, an interaction that first requires a personal, affective (what she calls "aesthetic") response. Many pedagogical theorists have since written about how to apply a "response-based" philosophy of literature teaching to the secondary classroom, including Robert Probst (1988) and Alan Purves, Theresa Rogers, and Anna Soter (1995). These authors give specific suggestions for applying reader-response theory to the classroom, including response writings, theme-based teaching, literature circles or small-group discussions, responding to popular media texts, and facilitating cultural critiques.

Narratives

In this chapter, we present four narratives that focus on the teaching of literature and reading. Past or present classroom teachers tell the stories, and experienced teachers of literature or teacher educators respond. These responses do not necessarily provide the "answers" for all scenarios similar to the ones narrated, but we hope that the stories, coupled with the responses, will help you think about your developing philosophy of teaching literature and reading and how you will use texts of various kinds with your future students.

The first narrative, "Where Is Your River? Reader Responses to *Huckleberry Finn*" tells the story of a high school teacher who relates a classic novel often taught in secondary schools to the lives of young adults. The second story, "Handing Over the Script: Using Images in the Literature Class," talks about teaching *To Kill a Mockingbird* to young adults and asking them to respond with a visual image, a drawing, instead of the normal paper-and-pencil quizzes or study guides. The third story, "The One That Didn't Work: Struggles with Literature Circles," narrates a teacher's attempt to use literature circles in her tenth-grade English class and the problems she had implementing the approach. The last narrative, "A Chilly Idea: A Tactile Approach to Teaching Literature," tells how one teacher brought an often-inaccessible text home to her students through tactile and kinesthetic stimulation.

Literature Narrative 1

The Adventures of Huckleberry Finn is often taught in high schools. Sometimes it is also the subject of controversy when students, parents, and administrators are troubled by the depiction of the African American character Jim and the racial epithet used to describe him. This teacher tells how he was able to move past these controversies (at least for a while) and help students feel a part of Huck's world. This narrative comes from an American literature class made up primarily of tenth graders in a school of about 1,700 students located in a small Wisconsin city.

> **Where Is Your River? Reader Responses to *Huckleberry Finn***
>
> We said there warn't no home like a raft, after all. Other places do seem so cramped up and smothery, but a raft don't. You feel mighty free and easy and comfortable on a raft.
>
> Mark Twain, *The Adventures of Huckleberry Finn*

Today's students face a fast-paced world and many modern stresses, along with the usual frustrations and concerns of adolescence. As my students and I read *The Adventures of Huckleberry Finn* and discussed the often negative influences of society both in the novel and in our current American culture, I formed the idea for a personal writing response that would, like Huck's refuge from the shore on the raft in the middle of the river, elicit "free and easy and comfortable" feelings from the student writers.

There is more than enough conflict, whether in fiction or real life, to write about, I thought; too many young writers, when invited to share their feelings, share stories of pain and struggle. While these stories provide a valuable and sometimes necessary outlet and certainly have their place, I wanted to encourage positive responses for this particular activity.

Since we had discussed the general theme of the river versus the shore in Twain's novel, I asked my students to answer these questions: Where is your "river"? Where do you feel, like Huck Finn, peaceful and happy and "comfortable"? From their answers, the students were to develop a piece of writing explaining their responses. As an example, I shared with them a writing model I had completed describing our family cabin and surrounding woods in northern Wisconsin near the Michigan border where I experience those "free and easy" feelings.

Later, as I sat at my desk and read the students' responses, I quietly rejoiced that these young people had their own places or memories that made them feel at peace. All of the writings were very much like the following examples:

> My river is not exactly a place. It is the feeling I have when dancing. And, although it's more of a mood, I do feel transported to my special dancing place in my mind. I become one with the dance. I will always find peacefulness when dancing.

> The one place that I think compares with Huck's raft on the river would be my room. When I am in my room, I can shut the door and shut out all of my problems at home or at school.

> The place I go that's like Huck's river is our barn. When I'm there, I am often alone with all the horses. It's like time stopping. There is a certain wonder that I feel when I get up on a horse.

> My "river" is actually a river. The Wisconsin River flows past the end of my backyard. Sometimes, when I'm stressed or up-

> set, I take out our paddleboat. This helps me think and relax.
> It's peaceful, just like it is for Huck.
>
> I saw in the student responses not only genuine connections
> to the literature but also personal expressions of positive experiences.
> And I hope that all readers, young and old, have their own "rivers."

A Teacher Responds

This narrative tells the story of a success, of a teacher asking students
to engage in a writing activity that has very positive results. I commend
the teacher on his willingness to allow students to respond personally
to classic literature. Texts like *Huckleberry Finn* can be difficult to teach
to adolescents. *Huck Finn* can seem anachronistic to students—completely alien to their experiences and lives, and therefore they can be
reluctant to read or respond to it with any depth. Add into the mix the
not unwarranted controversy surrounding the novel concerning the
frequent use of the word *nigger,* and teaching *Huck Finn* becomes even
more difficult.

Another thing that seems important here is that the teacher is
determined to help students focus on something positive about the book
instead of on the negative. In modern talk show culture, it is common-
place for people to tell horror stories of things gone wrong in their lives:
violence, abuse, pain, sadness, etc. While I think these negatives often
need to be told, where is the discussion of the positive, the good, and
the happy? Although teachers and readers must recognize that conflict
is often at the heart of any literary work, it is sometimes possible and,
as this teacher shows us, even desirable to focus on the positive. This
teacher asks his students to think about their own "rivers," their places
of peace and refuge, and he gets some marvelous student responses.

I think he could take this activity further in order to engage in
deeper analysis and criticism of *Huck Finn.* When the student writes
about "shutting out all my problems at home or school," for example,
discussion could focus on how and why Huck does a similar thing. What
are Huck's problems? To what extent are they caused by or reflected in
the time in which this fictional character is living? What happens on the
raft between Huck and Jim that can't or doesn't happen elsewhere?
Why? How is this a reflection of nineteenth-century, pre–Civil War
America? What happens when Huck and Jim leave the raft (as when
the student leaves her room)? In other words, these wonderful personal
connections can also be used to facilitate literary analysis and even social-cultural criticism. In this way, the teacher can direct students to a

discussion of the racial issues and themes central to the book. How, for example, does Huck and Jim's time on the raft provide a space for an expression of friendship impossible on the shore? How and why do their interactions again change when they return to land? What larger point might Twain have been trying to make about racial discrimination by placing the two settings in opposition? Many pedagogical theorists have argued that, regardless of the specific discussions in which students eventually engage, literary study begins with response (both making personal connections and giving opinions), moves to analysis and interpretation (taking apart and examining the chunks or pieces), and finally arrives at criticism (putting back together and linking/connecting to the larger world to see a greater significance). This teacher has begun this process in a positive way by asking a seemingly simple question: where is your river?

A Teacher Responds

This high school teacher creates an important opportunity for the students to engage with both *Huckleberry Finn* (the text) and Huck Finn (the character) when they are asked to consider their own experiences and ideas as they relate to Mark Twain's image of the Mississippi River. The students seize the chance to pause and reflect on a basic need we all have to seek refuge, safety, and comfort in the midst of complicated and challenging times. And in doing so, a nearly 120-year-old text finds new life in the hands of today's high school students.

With the text in their hands and an intriguing question to consider, the students find themselves placed in the position of being responsible for making meaning out of the confluence of the text and their own thoughts, rather than being given a particular interpretation of the text from their teacher. It's through their teacher's perceptive question that they set out on their journey toward becoming more sophisticated, thoughtful readers. In exploring the question of how readers make meaning from texts, Louise Rosenblatt (1978) posits, "The finding of meanings involves both the author's text and what the reader brings to it" (p. 14). In this case, the students make the most of their chance to pull up a chair, sit next to Twain, consider the very same issues he thought about as he wrote the book, and then make new meanings.

Sophisticated and able readers, of course, tend to make connections between more than just themselves and the text. Quite often it's our most engaged readers who also have the inclination and the patience to seek or see connections between the text, other works of literature, and the world at large. Leila Christenbury (2000) provides a framework for thinking about the pedagogy of questioning techniques when she explains her vision of the questioning circle and dense questions, wherein she notes the need for readers to consider how their own ideas and the world at large intersect and interact with the text at hand (pp. 254–55). Perhaps these students would have welcomed the challenge of considering the idea of rivers as they have encountered them in other works of literature or on film. The teacher's provocative, initial question easily could have served as a springboard to talk about the river as a literary archetype, one that carries a multiplicity of associations and connections throughout countless other novels, short stories, and poems. One easily could bring into such a discussion Harriet Beecher Stowe's treatment of the Ohio River in *Uncle Tom's Cabin*, Willa Cather's portrayal of a small river in Nebraska in her story "The Enchanted Bluff," or Langston Hughes's perception of numerous rivers in his poem "The Negro Speaks of Rivers." If and when students have the opportunity to see the connections between the work of literature at hand and other works, they begin to see stories and poems in a larger, richer context.

The larger, richer context also brings with it a certain literary double-edged sword. That is to say, students who are invited to consider every angle of a particular literary image not only begin to see how that particular motif might be extended, but they are also more likely to sense that the image is more complicated and complex than they first thought. In doing so, students can become more adept at challenging both the text and their own initial interpretations. By asking students, as I am suggesting here, to think about "river" as a literary archetype, they are likely to see that Huck Finn's river might be more complicated than it first appears and that Twain might not have intended it to be understood simply and solely as a place of refuge and safety. As the novel moves along, it's the river, of course, that not only protects Huck but also carries him deeper and deeper into the South, into greater peril and more dangerous situations. This would be a good time to remind students that the raft bore two passengers the length of the adventure, and Jim likely had a much different perspective on the raft and its direction than did Huck. By the end of the novel, Huck abandons the civilization *and* the river altogether to "light out for the Territory, ahead of the rest."

To be sure, approaching the text in this manner ultimately works against the teacher's stated intention of keeping an absolutely positive focus on the idea of the river as a place of refuge. This approach would serve as an option, however, for extending the students' understanding of the river's function within the story. Doing so would allow students to explore the imagery of the river in all its richness and complexity—within the text of the story, the mind of the reader, and the world of ideas at large. The students who are ready and willing and sufficiently patient to complicate the idea of the river both within and outside of the text might appreciate the chance to move beyond the confining banks of the river, just as Huck chooses to do at the end of his adventure.

For Further Discussion

1. Thinking back to your experiences as a middle school, high school, and college student, what role do you think personal response plays in literary study? Do you think a personal response or personal "connection" is essential for eventual analysis and criticism of a text? Why or why not?

2. Do you think that reading "positive" texts and responding in positive ways are important activities for adolescents? Why or why not?

3. Can you think of any young adult novels that address similar themes or issues and thus might be paired with *Huckleberry Finn* (in order to facilitate its teaching)? How do you see them connecting thematically?

Learning Activities

1. Practice leading a literary discussion with your students or peers about a short passage from a text of your choice. Write down in advance possible questions to ask them, but also think about what ideas or concepts you would like them to consider by the end of the discussion. Think about structuring the discussion in an inductive way so that you help your students or peers construct these ideas on their own.

2. Draw a diagram that represents your philosophy of teaching literature and include the following approaches from which to address or analyze a text: personal response, historical background information, author's biographical information, social-cultural critique or criticism (i.e., issues of gender, class, race/ethnicity), and close readings of the language of texts. In this diagram, show which of these you think is the most important to teaching or approaching a text by giving it more space, and then visually demonstrate the importance you place on the others in a similar way. Then share this diagram of your literature teaching philosophy with peers or colleagues and talk about your philosophical similarities and differences.

Literature Narrative 2

More and more often, teachers are using the visual in order to facilitate student thought and help students respond to texts in richer ways. Visual thinking is not a new idea. Rudolf Arnheim (1969) wrote much about visual processes of thought, and more recently Howard Gardner (1983) included the visual thinker in his enumerated "intelligences" or ways in which individuals learn or approach new material. The teacher who tells the following story taps into the power of the image when teaching *To Kill a Mockingbird* by Harper Lee. This narrative is written from the perspective of a first-year teacher.

Handing Over the Script: Using Images in the Literature Class

To say that I was a little nervous during my first year of teaching would be a colossal understatement. Every night my stomach churned as I tried to plan the "foolproof" lesson. I scripted everything down to the minutest detail, determined to be so prepared that I wouldn't have to improvise anything. Veteran teachers with whom I worked chuckled at my obsessive habit. They would try to comfort me, saying, "Oh, someday you'll be able to walk into the classroom without anything written down." I didn't believe them.

In industry they say, "Necessity is the mother of invention." In teaching, it's exasperation that gives birth to creative ideas. My students had been reading *To Kill a Mockingbird*. We were through the first four or five chapters and class discussions were going nowhere. I had given the students study guides, quizzes, and journal entries, none of which produced anything more than the usual pat answers and simplistic responses. As usual, I had the day's lesson scripted out, but I just couldn't face another fifty minutes of long pauses, sleepy faces, and distracted chatter in the back of the room.

When the students finally took their seats as the bell rang, I passed out a blank sheet of paper. I said, "I want you to draw a picture of Boo Radley." I held my breath for the groans and yawns, but to my surprise, real interest and even a little excitement actually charged the room. Students dug into book bags for pencils. I heard mumbles of "Oh, cool!" or "This is fun." A few looked dumbfounded and pained. Drawing wasn't something you did in English class. I assured them they could use stick figures or simple sketches and that they wouldn't have to share them with the class. After twenty minutes, I asked for volunteers to put their drawings on the board so we could decide who had drawn the best likeness of Boo. Real discussion and debate erupted. Some students felt that certain drawings completely misrepresented the Boo they had pictured in their minds. "He wouldn't be smoking a cigarette!"; "You made him too young."; "Why did you put scissors in his hand?" With each of these comments, I asked why or why not, leading students back to the text to support their conclusions about Boo. I also discovered who had been reading carefully and who hadn't, and those individuals weren't necessarily the same students who had been doing well on the quizzes and homework. Students had to gather their books quickly as class ended, more eager to read on and find out the "real" story about Boo. I breathed a satisfied sigh of relief. I didn't need the script. As long as I had a destination, I could improvise, make detours, and discover shortcuts to getting my students excited about a story.

I also learned that I need to help my students *see* the text. In the thirteen years since that first class, I have researched the connections between teaching visualization strategies and reading comprehension. "Read the movie in your head" has become my mantra. Now when we read *To Kill a Mockingbird*, I often ask students to stop and draw what is happening in the story. I also include assignments in which groups of students storyboard entire chapters, as filmmakers do before they actually go into production. When the students discuss what to include in each frame of their storyboard, I see them paying closer attention to the text. But we also discuss the filmmaker's prerogative to create a script with some details that may not be included in the text but that will help convey its main ideas and themes. In other words, the students begin to quite literally *draw* their own inferences about the facial expressions of characters, the set details, and the camera distance: would the scene be shot as a close up or a long shot? Paying special attention to the picture the author wants projected onto the reader's mind helps students think visually in their own writing so that they create "movies in the head" of their own readers.

All of this began that day I decided not to follow the script and finally let my students create their own.

A Teacher Responds

There are so many interesting ideas within this narrative I hardly know where to begin. This teacher talks about a couple of things I want to address: the difficulty of being a new teacher and using visual representation to respond to literature. First, the issue of the new teacher's confidence (or lack thereof).

A new teacher undergoes a great deal of stress and change as she moves from being a university student to a high school or middle school teacher. Many of the problems and stressors are related to issues of identity and authority. As Deborah Britzman (1991) writes, "So at first glance, becoming a teacher may mean becoming someone you are not. It is this dual struggle that works to construct the student teacher as the site of conflict" (p. 4). How is becoming a teacher like becoming someone you are not? It happens when a young teacher strives to take on a teacher persona or own an identity as a teacher that he or she is initially uncomfortable with. The teacher in this narrative describes her struggles with this identity development her first year of teaching and how as part of her struggle she feels more confident writing explicit notes about what she is to do or say in a classroom on any particular day. This is her "script" as a teacher, just as an actor learns a script to take on a role in a play or movie. This is not to say that taking notes or writing lesson plans is something that only young teachers do; on the contrary, good planning often requires writing things down. This teacher's story, however, demonstrates that sometimes good teachers deviate from their notes, from the script, when the classroom moment dictates or when students seem to need or demand another approach.

Second, this teacher describes her belief in the power of visual thinking when she asks students to draw a picture of Boo and then again later in her career when she requires students to create storyboards of different chapters in *To Kill a Mockingbird*. Visual thinking is documented as an important cognitive act. Rudolf Arnheim (1969) was among the first to argue that "visual perception is a cognitive activity" (p. v). He goes on to say, "cognitive operations called thinking are not the privilege of mental processes above and beyond perception but the essential ingredients of perception itself" (p. 13). Arnheim's understanding of the image and of focused and reflective viewing as both a form of thinking and of expressing thought was relatively new in his day. Others since Arnheim, however, have valued visualization as a viable form of thought, including Howard Gardner, who in his book *Frames of Mind: The Theory of Multiple Intelligences* (1983) identifies "spatial intelligence" as the ability "to perceive the visual world accurately, to perform transformations and modifications upon one's initial perceptions, and to be able to re-create aspects of one's visual experience" (p. 173). Thus, this teacher is supported in her effort to recognize visual thinking and see value in asking students to visualize characters, events, and so on. The pictures the students draw of Boo are directly linked in the teacher's narrative to class discussion about the character: who he was, why he acted as he did, and so forth. And even better, the pictures led to debate about these motivations and descriptors. Because of the initial drawing activity, students engaged in arguments about the character and the text.

One final note: a related but also useful activity is readers' theater. In this activity, students read aloud "parts" and, using minimal props and actions, dramatize scenes from prose or poetic works. Readers' theater allows students not only to visualize the motions characters might go through in a particular scene but also to take on the persona of a character and enact these visualizations. This enactment could lead to deeper understanding of the characters' motivations that might lead to a more comprehensive understanding of the text.

A Teacher Responds

This particular narrative shows how one beginning teacher's practice evolved from a stance characterized by a sense of safety to a stance of risk-taking. Early in her career, this beginning teacher found safety in being obsessively prepared with scripted lesson plans that enabled her to predict almost every aspect of a lesson. Ultimately, desperation enabled her to take the risk of spontaneity, which enabled her students to engage with texts in meaningful, reflective, and thoughtful ways. As a result of the teacher's shift from a scripted to an improvisational approach, an important thing happens with the students. As this beginning teacher loosens the reins a bit and offers the students an opportunity to interact with the text in ways they could not with study guides, quizzes, and journal entries, they engage in meaningful thinking, talking, and reflecting about the text. The teacher writes, "Real discussion and debate erupted." Although she says that she led "students back to the text to support their conclusions," I argue that the students led her. By allowing them to engage with the text through their drawings, the teacher actually relinquishes control, and the students lead her through their meaning making, as it should be in a student/reader-centered literature classroom.

Through her reflections, the teacher was able to document her learning in the narrative: "I also learned that I need to help my students *see* the text." This is important for two reasons. First, it shows that given time and reflection, teachers—even beginning teachers—can, through intentional contemplation, critically examine their practice and their learning as professionals. Second, she realized that her students needed to somehow "see" the text differently in order to engage in more meaningful conversations about it, and she realized it was her responsibility as the teacher to help them do so. Robert Probst (1988), Louise Rosenblatt (1978, 1982, 1983), Frank Smith (1978, 1988), and others who subscribe to the psycholinguistic perspective (Goodman, 1996; Scholes, 1985) have taught us that meaningful, engaging interactions with texts occur when students understand that they have an integral role in the reading of texts. Likewise, Jeffrey Wilhelm (1995) argues that we must show students, especially reluctant and struggling readers, how to engage with texts by offering them a variety of creative, innovative ways of interacting with texts and by granting them the freedom to make meaning with and about texts. Social constructivism (Dewey, 1938; Phillips, 1995; Vygotsky, 1962, 1987), with its assumption that knowledge is socially constructed and contextually situated, seems to be at the core of Wilhelm's work and also grounds this teacher's decision to create a situation in which students can draw from their personal experiences and beliefs as well as have the opportunity to interact with one another in small groups. According to Wilhelm (1995),

> By instead focusing our instruction and support on the construction of meaning, the classroom can become a place where students not only produce and share meanings, but a place where they share ways of reading and being with text, becoming aware in the process of their own strategies and those of others. (p. 11)

Writing is often used as a tool for enabling student engagement. Composition theorists for years have asserted that writing provides students a medium through which to construct meaning (Elbow, 1973; Emig, 1971; Moffett & Wagner, 1992; Murray, 1982, 1985; Newkirk, 1990). Writing offers students opportunities to make personal connections and reach higher levels of engagement that encourage purposeful response. Through writing, students can communicate their thoughts, opinions, interpretations, feelings, and criticism of what they read. The teacher in this narrative uses writing in concert with students' drawings and group collaboration. For her students, especially the reluctant writers, this was a stroke of genius.

Looking back on her experience as a beginning teacher, this English teacher was able to critically examine how her transformation began and speculate about the source of her creativity. She writes, "In teaching, it's exasperation that gives birth to creative ideas." Beginning and experienced teachers alike feel exasperated and frustrated when it seems everything they try falls flat and lessons or activities fail to engage students in meaningful and powerful ways. Just as we ask our students to move outside their comfort zones to try something new or to look at something from a different perspective, we teachers also must be willing to venture outside our comfort zone, take a risk, and relinquish control to our students. This teacher did just that, and she reaped the benefits as she enjoyed a class rich with engaged thought and conversation.

For Further Discussion

1. What do you think it means to be a secondary English teacher? How would you define such an individual? What qualities do you think an English teacher should exhibit? After considering these questions, write about your past, present, or future induction into the profession and how difficult (or easy) it has been or you think it will be to assume this professional identity.

2. Some educators would argue that drawing a picture is not a valid, intellectual response to a text. Do you agree or disagree? Why?

3. What is the difference between a classroom discussion and a question-and-answer session? When might each of these be useful? Why?

Learning Activities

1. Think of a text that you have read in the last month or two and create a visual response to it. Choose any visual form that appeals to you: an idea or concept cluster, a drawing of a character or individual in the text, a map of the setting of the story, a symbolic representation of a theme, etc. Then, if possible, discuss your visual response with a peer or colleague and think about how your thoughts or feelings about the text were changed (or not changed) because of the activity.

2. Working in a small group, brainstorm at least five ways you could integrate images into your future or current secondary English curriculum. How might you incorporate visual thinking into effective literature instruction?

Literature Narrative 3

Sometimes, what seem like good ideas do not work out so well in real classrooms. Are there certain activities or approaches that might sound like good ideas in university classes but that just do not work in reality? Or are there ways we can modify these approaches to make them more effective and successful? The following story narrates one teacher's experiences with literature circles in a tenth-grade class in a midsize Pennsylvania town.

The One That Didn't Work: Struggles with Literature Circles

About three years ago, before I had ever heard of literature circles, I decided to have my nonacademic tenth-grade class work on novels in small groups. I had purchased ten copies of half a dozen titles geared for high-interest, low-ability reading. I created study guides to accompany each title, chapter by chapter, and developed possible final project choices that I thought were broad enough to be used with any of the texts. These included basic oral reporting and "performances" as well as posters and bulletin boards. Students were also expected to keep a reading journal, with which they had already gained experience during our short story unit.

To start things off, I gave a minisummary of each of the titles. Students then divided themselves into groups based on the titles they were interested in reading. No group had more then six students or fewer than four, and a couple of novels were not chosen at all. I gave the class a due date for the novels to be finished, handed out study guides and noted that these would be collected with the final project, and gave each group a blank calendar of class periods so they could break down the reading according to their own timetable. I did not assign roles to anyone, basically because I was not familiar with literature circles and the accompanying roles as described by Harvey Daniels (1994).

The first day, I asked the groups to scan their novels and to give me an approximate timetable for their reading. They knew they would have class time each day until the final date but that they would not necessarily have all period every day (we were on an eighty-eight-minute block schedule). During the class periods, group members could read aloud to one another or read silently, work on study questions or on the final projects, or generally discuss what they had read. I was available to all groups for consultation and frequently checked on overall progress.

This activity didn't work the way I would have liked. I think the problem was due in part to the composition of the class. This was a tenth-grade class with a high proportion of repeat students. Although these students often did not do assignments, I thought the work might get done this time if they had more control of the material and assignments. The class also had a high absentee rate. Some students came to school only sporadically. Others came to school but were discipline problems and often ended up in an alternate class for

▶

days or weeks at a time. A couple of students were frequently in out-of-school suspension. This absentee problem left a handful of students in each group to carry the load. It was not unusual for a group to have only two members present. I tried to allow for this in evaluating the assignment by noting the frequency of absences and the participation of group members when present. I also had group members fill out evaluations on one another at the end of the project. Interestingly, a few students rated their group members highly even if they hadn't been present throughout much of the assignment.

While the class as a whole was exposed to more novels than we would have had time to cover together, I was disappointed with the attempt. It seemed as though the same students who had previously failed to complete work assigned as part of the whole class had also failed to complete work even when they had choices about the time frame and, to some degree, about the type of activities related to the novel.

A Teacher Responds

Jacqueline McWilliams Chappel (1998) paraphrases Harvey Daniels's description of literature circles as follows:

> Literature circles are student-led, small-group discussions of a book that all group members have read. The teacher briefly reviews the books children may choose from, each child reads a book of his or her choice, and participates in a discussion group with others who chose the same book. (pp. 125–26)

Chappel goes on to describe how the students take on different "roles" as a way to contribute to the group, roles that include "discussion director, illustrator, connector, word wizard, and so forth" (1998, p. 126). Oftentimes, the literature circles unit ends with a group project representing the students' collective, often creative, response to the text. This teacher gave book talks prior to having students choose texts, gave groups the freedom to set their own reading schedules, asked students to complete written assignments related to the books, and also required them to have small-group discussions. She seems to have followed Daniels's guidelines for literature circles almost to a tee, even though she had not heard of them prior to her attempt. I am impressed by her creative thinking and the risk-taking that allowed her to try with reluctant students an activity that she hoped would increase their motivation and their learning. But this teacher was still unhappy with the way the project turned out.

As she notes, some of the problems would be difficult for her to solve by herself without school or parental help: absentee rates, disciplinary infractions, and a general apathy about passing courses. I think, however, there are some things the teacher might have done that could have improved the chances of literature circles working in this tenth-grade class. Going back to Daniels, I think he would agree that assigning roles is key to the success of literature circles. In his book, co-written with Marilyn Bizar, called *Methods That Matter: Six Structures for Best Practice Classrooms* (1998), Daniels describes how one teacher "taught" her students these roles, gave them concrete directions for enacting them, and created for herself more specific ways to evaluate their performance. The "discussion director" for example, is the person whose responsibility it is to come up with questions to begin the group discussion on any particular day. The teacher discusses the difference between "open" and "closed" questions and encourages discussion directors to write down as many open questions as possible. The "passage master" picks parts of the story that would be effective when read aloud to the rest of the group; the passage master also must identify why he or she chose those passages. In this way, each student has a role (these roles may rotate during the unit), and the role has not only an oral component but also a written one that can be easily assessed. One of this teacher's problems seems to be student accountability; the students don't complete the literature circle tasks with diligence and motivation, so perhaps the measures discussed in Daniels's book might increase accountability and hence the quality of the discussions that take place. In addition to the accountability measures already established by the teacher (e.g., reading journals, study guides, and final projects), having students play specific roles could enhance and balance the students' self-evaluations.

A Teacher Responds

This narrative offers insight into the real-world problems and complexities of teaching. This teacher attempted to be creative in her approach to teaching literature by using literature circles. She incorporated many of the elements deemed necessary by Daniels (1994) for a successful literature circle learning experience, including choice, student responsibility, and the importance of discussion. She made the choice to make students more responsible for their own learning. Thus, she thought she had created a space for increased student interest and engagement. Yet she was disappointed with the outcome. I think it is important to note that several factors beyond the teacher's control, especially those related to students' absence from class, affected the literature circles approach in ways she had not foreseen.

There is little doubt that the teacher learned much from this experience, which confirms the power of this particular narrative. There are, however, other lessons to be learned from such an experience. While this teacher could have made instructional changes, as discussed in the previous response, there are other issues that go beyond the immediate context of this or any other teaching and learning event. Moreover, these important issues go beyond the realm of English studies.

I would venture to propose that those students who were not present or not participative during the literature circle activities for the variety of reasons listed by this teacher, including suspension, truancy, and simply a failure to complete the work, became disengaged from the promise of schooling long before they entered this classroom. As educators we need to consider the underlying reasons for chronic absenteeism, truancy, discipline problems, and lack of student motivation for engaging in certain academic tasks. Much research has been done regarding why some students do not engage in the academic process over the course of their careers in school. In *It's Never Too Late* (1995), Janet Allen states:

> Previously, these students had no reason to be motivated. Weiner cites his claim that "in our culture two sources of motivation are most dominant: achievement and social recognition." These students could not tell me of any times they had felt successful or received social recognition for their academic achievements. In fact, for years they had been characterized, and characterized themselves, as "failures, slow learners, learning disabled, special ed, remedial, and resource." These characterizations, and their accompanying traits, had edged these students into a state that Seligman terms "learned helplessness." They had entered my classroom last August expecting nothing. (p. 157)

Dale Schunk (1991) also contends that some students attribute their struggles to a lack of ability and begin to believe that their hard work is futile, resulting in a lack of motivation to attempt or engage in academic tasks. The lack of confidence in one's own ability and potential often results in behaviors similar to those described by this teacher and which had negative implications for her lessons.

One must wonder how many times the students who negatively affected their groups' literature circle performance had similar opportunities to take control of their own learning in the past or even during other class periods that same year. Especially when considering struggling students, we as teachers must question why some students continue to practice what we often perceive to be academically destructive behaviors.

Unfortunately, many other teachers have learned the same painful lesson and, because of or before seriously considering the influence of these outside factors, have discarded such new and innovative approaches that make students more responsible for and involved in constructing their own meanings about literature. Obviously there are no easy answers. But I would encourage this teacher not to lose faith in working to engage students, despite the fact that the very thing that research and even students themselves tell us makes a difference—choice—did not work well the first time she attempted to include it. As indicated in the previous response, students need to be provided with numerous opportunities to learn how to use such an approach themselves. In many cases, teachers trying out new strategies and approaches will find that their students have little or no experience with these activities. Peter Johnston and Richard Allington (2002), for example, contend that many students who are remediated in lower-level language arts classes have simply been exposed to too many isolated skill-and-drill types of exercises rather than introduced to meaningful learning opportunities. In many cases, when they are put in situations requiring different skills and critical thinking, they have no idea what they are doing or why. Therefore, it is crucial that we give students the time they need to learn about their new roles and responsibilities, as well as about the new instructional process in which they are asked to engage.

I would urge this teacher to stay the course, continue trying new approaches and strategies, and give students the time and the instruction necessary to get accustomed to the idea that they can actually have some responsibility for their own learning and be interested and engaged in the work at the same time. I would also encourage all teachers in all content areas and at every grade level to help these challenging students find reasons to engage in classroom activities that are relevant to their lives and to empower them by giving them a voice in the decisions surrounding their own learning. As well, and perhaps more important, I would encourage this teacher to find ways to continue working through the complicated issues present in every classroom that make being a creative and student-centered teacher difficult at times, to say the least. Working toward that goal early on in students' school experiences can have tremendous impact on students' attendance, attitude, and achievement throughout their academic careers.

For Further Discussion

1. What skills or concepts do you think literature circles teach secondary students? Can they teach these skills or concepts more effectively than traditional approaches? Why or why not?

2. Think about secondary students' development. Jean Piaget (1926) sees adolescents moving from concrete to abstract thought. Lev Vygotsky (1962) values social interaction as a way of internalizing and utilizing metacognition, or thinking about thinking. Do you think that literature circles are well or poorly suited to this developmental stage of life? Why or why not?

3. The second responder talked at length about possible reasons why some students choose not to attend or participate in school. One reason she suggested is that students may not be comfortable with activities that allow them choice or freedom in how they approach or complete a task. How might an English teacher help students become more comfortable engaging in independent thought and action? How might a teacher support students as they learn how to take control of their own learning?

Learning Activities

1. Participate in a book group or reading group and try to imitate or incorporate some of Daniels's (1994) strategies for literature circles. Then consider how such social engagement with the text changed your interpretation or response to it.

2. Consider the role of choice in learning. Do you think having a choice increases motivation? Examine this question by conducting a very small study in a secondary classroom. During a field experience or in your own classroom, ask a student to first write a short response to a particular prompt; the next day, ask him or her to *choose* one of two prompts to write a response to. Do you observe any difference in how the student responds to each requirement? If so, what is the difference? You may even ask the student if he or she felt more motivated to do the activity when choice was involved.

Literature Narrative 4

This story recounts one teacher's attempt to get students involved in the Alexsandr Solzhenitsyn novella *One Day in the Life of Ivan Denisovich*. The teacher uses the motif of "cold" to help students unaccustomed to frigid weather understand a major theme of the book and learn something about themselves. This story takes place in a secondary school in Manila, Philippines.

A Chilly Idea: A Tactile Approach to Teaching Literature

The concept of cold permeated *One Day in the Life of Ivan Denisovich*. I wanted my students to understand the cold—so cold there would be frost on the inside of windows. As Solzhenitsyn writes, "Where could you get warm in a place like this, with the windows iced over and the white cobwebs of frost all along the huge barracks where the walls joined the ceiling" (p. 3). Most of my twenty students had been born and raised in the hot, humid tropics of the Philippines. They understood heat and humidity, but cold was somewhat foreign to them. If they did not understand cold, they would not understand the entire book.

Because the concept of cold is a recurring one in the text, it had been assigned to a student to "cover" in a class presentation. In a brainstorming discussion I held with her, she came up with several ideas to help take the students through the book. I asked her if she had any ideas about how to make the students experience cold. With some prompting, she observed the air conditioner in the room, and she also knew that ice was cold. She added some clothing limitations and a barefoot requirement, and her presentation was ready.

The class met during first period, so I arrived at school early the designated day, turned up the AC as high as possible, and waited for my student leader. She had arranged for several "guards" at the door who made sure everyone shed clothing until just decent. Barefoot, the students entered the room and were handed an ice cube in a Baggie with instructions to hold the ice until it melted in their hands. Additionally, there were buckets of ice water on the floor. Each student had to put one foot in a bucket and one foot on the rapidly chilling floor. As students got cold and said so, the entire class was instructed to walk around the perimeter of the room, holding on to the ice cube and marching in parade formation.

Eventually the ice melted, and the students were told to take their feet out of the water, dry them, put on shoes, and debrief. My student in charge of the "cold" led the discussion. Many of the students dramatically shared their growing awareness that they hadn't been able to think; the cold had seeped into their heads and made it difficult to pay attention. Having been cold themselves helped the students to more fully grasp the significance of cold in Solzhenitsyn's novella.

In the semester evaluation, most of the students commented

on that particular activity. They felt they had learned more in one encounter than in the many other activities they had done in high school. Additionally, they were delighted with the participatory nature of the activity. Finally, they felt they had been involved with the decisions because the entire period had been student led, including the discussion afterward. I too was pleased. The students took what could have been simply another class discussion and turned it into a profound learning experience.

A Teacher Responds

My first reaction is wow! What a scene! It is no easy feat to generate excitement over characters, setting, and themes in a novel. Here we have a classroom of barefoot students trying to physically connect with this story's mood by sacrificing their own comfort. Activities like this don't occur very often. It's no wonder that students list this activity as one of their most memorable events.

This dynamic activity is powerful in its design. The fact that it is student led offers powerful lessons in leadership and independence. But how much of this was the student's design? I wonder if this is a good example of a student-led activity or a bit of puppetry with the teacher's ideas coming out of the student's mouth. Or does it matter? The student certainly led the discussion and organized the day's events. This in itself is freeing for students, especially in a day filled with static activities.

Another question is how much learning actually occurred. Is this experiential for the sake of the experience, or is it adequately connected back to the novel? What are students asked to do to relate their kinesthetic experience to the context of that novel? This is especially a concern because students reported that they had trouble thinking due to the cold. If the students are feeling the mind-numbing effects of the cold, how effective can the discussion be? Would a follow-up with a writing prompt be more helpful in bringing students down from the rush of this event?

This reminds me of my own attempts at experiential learning, which resulted in various degrees of success. One plan was for my class to walk to the river in conjunction with reading *Siddhartha* by Hermann Hesse. Once there, we would sit and listen to the water just as Siddhartha had done waiting for enlightenment. But the students were so excited to be outside that they could hardly contain themselves. The environment inspired chaos rather than Nirvana. The lesson of quiet listening required more self-discipline than my students could muster.

Perhaps if such learning experiences were not such a rarity, students would be able to adjust more easily. Literature teachers endeavoring to reach the kinesthetic learner take the risk of swimming in chaos, but that risk is worth the attempt. The impact of feeling an event, touching the lives within a novel, and doing rather than hearing or reading about an activity cannot be overlooked.

A Teacher Responds

Truly, such texts as *A Day in the Life of Ivan Denisovich* must be contextualized environmentally. This English teacher chooses to emphasize the tactile response attendant upon life in bone-chilling climates. It is an interesting stance to adopt and would create a memorable association for students' empathic perspective. Attempting to manipulate tactile responses presents both benefits and setbacks, though. Our tactile senses are our slowest to adapt, probably our least reliable, and are not as strongly attached to memory as olfactory and visual senses are. These facts highlight a need to explore tactile responses further and ensure novelty of the activity.

In light of the inherent difficulties connected to buckets of water, disrobing, and Baggies of ice, perhaps a more generalizable emphasis should accompany the "chilly" idea. Solzhenitsyn's work provides a perfect literary sample for "ecocriticism." First, as David Mazel (2000) writes, students might work toward *ecological identity*, establishing their own and recognizing others'. This involves all of us consciously seeing ourselves in relation to nature, "in reference to nature, as living and breathing beings connected to the rhythms of the earth, the bio-geochemical cycles, the grand and complex diversity of ecological systems" (p. 16).

Working to meet this state lends itself to interdisciplinary activities, especially connections with science, art, social studies, and health and safety, perhaps even in culture studies of foreign languages. Establishing a foundation of ecological identities is best achieved through primary research: gathering personal histories, mapmaking, interviewing, sifting through archives of photos and records, physically experiencing natural settings, maybe even altering the environment through organized programs in the community such as cleanups and tree plantings.

Ecocriticism then provides a link between the students' own ecological identities and those of the text's author and characters. This focus on relationships between literature and the physical environment can be said to have "officially" begun in 1996 when the first ecocriticism volume, *The Ecocriticism Reader: Landmarks in Literary Ecology* (Glotfelty & Fromm), was published. In conferences and in publications, the emphasis is on analysis of nature writing and wilderness literature. Recently, however, critics and authors have been more and more interested in gazing at all sorts of literature through this lens. Adopting an ecological perspective may be excellent preparation for modern students as well as prove to be of high interest and motivation. Topics range within a broad and vibrant spectrum, including such ideas as monstrous creatures of films, Robert Frost and New England objects, swamps and poetry, Virginia Woolf and the landscape, and "botanical discourse" in the works of Harriet Beecher Stowe.

While some teachers may not be interested in putting so much stress on environment in a study of Solzhenitsyn's novella, at least some attention to ecological identity and ecocriticism should be rewarding. From there, students who are ready for the next challenge can leap ahead and back historically to views on the spirit of place. It should be worth the trip!

For Further Discussion

1. Drawing from your own experiences as a student and a teacher, do you think there are any types of activities—physical, emotional, or intellectual—that are inappropriate in a secondary school English class? If so, what are they and why are they inappropriate?

2. Do you believe that the physical senses (sight, sound, touch, taste, smell) are linked to thoughts and feelings? In other words, does the experience of certain sensations increase the likelihood of certain thoughts and/or feelings? If you believe this is true, how then could that affect or influence the teaching of literature?

3. What other ways could you see using literary texts to encourage ecological criticism or sensitivity? What particular text do you have in mind?

Learning Activities

1. In a small group, brainstorm a list of four to five bodily or kinesthetic activities you could use in the literature classroom to facilitate discussion of a work of literature. How would you initiate these activities? How would you execute them?

2. Conduct some research about ecological issues or problems in your community. How could these issues be integrated into classroom projects for your students?

In Closing

This chapter has covered a lot of ground concerning the teaching of literature and reading. We have outlined some best practices and some major controversies and also shared some stories from real teachers about literature instruction, both successful and unsuccessful, in their classrooms. We hope these stories, as well as the accompanying information and responses, will help you as you continue to think about and develop your own philosophy of teaching literature in the secondary school.

As a concluding activity, write a philosophy of teaching literature. Write a short (no more than one page) statement of philosophy. Try to begin to answer some of the following questions as you describe your current or future classroom practices in teaching literature and reading and the beliefs that guide them:

1. Why do I think my students should read literature?
2. What is the role of young adult and classic texts in my classroom?
3. How will I facilitate literature discussions?
4. How will I incorporate visual, as well as linear, thinking and response?
5. How will I incorporate a variety of types of texts and texts by and about diverse groups of people?
6. How will I assist struggling readers when they need help?
7. How will I move students through response to analysis and criticism?

Additional Texts about the Teaching of Literature

Books and Journals

The ALAN Review.
This journal is a publication of the Assembly on Literature for Adolescents of the National Council of Teachers of English and is published three times a year. Members of NCTE who are also members of ALAN receive the journal. It contains articles and reviews of young adult literature.

Alvermann, Donna E. (Ed). (2002). *Adolescents and Literacies in a Digital World.* New York: Peter Lang.

> This is a collection of essays about the importance of digital technologies and media in today's youth culture as well as in second-

ary education. This book is a scholarly exploration of the "new literacies."

Alvermann, Donna E., Jennifer S. Moon, and Margaret C. Hagood. (1999). *Popular Culture in the Classroom: Teaching and Researching Critical Media Literacy.* Newark, DE: International Reading Association and Chicago: National Reading Conference.

Alvermann, Moon, and Hagood define what is meant by "critical media literacy" and then give practical suggestions and advice for engaging real students in such learning.

Appleman, Deborah. (2000). *Critical Encounters in High School English: Teaching Literary Theory to Adolescents.* New York: Teachers College Press and Urbana IL: National Council of Teachers of English.

Appleman discusses how teaching literary theory and criticism to high schools students can help them be better thinkers and readers and more open-minded individuals. She includes discussion of reader-response theory, Marxist theory, feminist theory, and deconstruction.

Atwell, Nancie. (1998). *In the Middle: New Understandings about Writing, Reading, and Learning* (2nd ed.). Portsmouth, NH: Boynton/Cook.

Atwell describes her "reading workshop" approach to teaching reading in which students select books, engage in silent reading during class time, learn reading processes through teacher-taught minilessons, and conference individually with teachers about their reading progress.

Carey-Webb, Allen. (2001). *Literature and Lives: A Response-Based, Cultural Studies Approach to Teaching English.* Urbana, IL: National Council of Teachers of English.

Carey-Webb provides theoretical and pedagogical justification for and examples of combining reader response– and cultural studies–based approaches to teaching literature.

Donelson, Kenneth L., and Alleen Pace Nilsen. (1997). *Literature for Today's Young Adults* (5th ed.). New York: Longman.

This is a textbook about the genre of young adult literature—what it is and how and why to teach it in secondary schools. Also included are discussions of different types of YA literature and the developmental level of adolescence.

Karolides, Nicholas J. (Ed.). (2000). *Reader Response in Secondary and College Classrooms*. Mahwah, NJ: Erlbaum.

This collection of essays (including one by Robert Probst) offers ideas on how reader-response theory can work in real classrooms.

Langer, Judith A. (1995). *Envisioning Literature: Literary Understanding and Literature Instruction*. New York: Teachers College Press.

Langer describes her "envisionment-building" approach to teaching literature that considers interpretation a never-ending process that involves the student responder in making new meaning (personal and literary) through engagement with texts. Langer describes how "scaffolding" literature discussions (building on students' prior knowledge) can help in this envisionment process.

Monseau, Virginia R. (1996). *Responding to Young Adult Literature*. Portsmouth, NH: Boynton/Cook.

Monseau gives specific suggestions for facilitating student response and thinking about young adult texts. She includes examples of responses from real students and focuses on how responding to young adult texts can facilitate critical thought.

Monseau, Virginia R., and Gary M. Salvner (Eds.). (2000). *Reading Their World: The Young Adult Novel in the Classroom*. Portsmouth, NH: Boynton/Cook.

This collection of essays focuses on various issues in the teaching of young adult literature, including how to deal with censors and how to engage students in critiquing novels through feminist, multicultural, and other critical lenses. The book comes with a searchable CD that includes almost 2,000 reviews of YA books.

Moore, John Noell. (1997). *Interpreting Young Adult Literature: Literary Theory in the Secondary Classroom*. Portsmouth NH: Boynton/Cook.

Moore takes several young adult books and applies different critical strategies to them, including formalism, cultural studies, and deconstruction. These critical readings are intended as models for secondary students and teachers. Moore's text is one of very few books that subjects YA literature to critical analysis.

Robb, Laura. (2000). *Teaching Reading in Middle School*. New York: Scholastic.

Robb, a thirty-five-year veteran of middle school teaching, discusses how to go about teaching reading effectively to middle school students. She includes many practical suggestions for teaching reading, including how to teach comprehension strategies that can increase students' motivation to read, and supports these suggestions with theory and research.

Smith, Michael W., and Jeffrey D. Wilhelm. (2002). *"Reading Don't Fix No Chevys": Literacy in the Lives of Young Men.* Portsmouth, NH: Heinemann.

This book reports on research conducted with dozens of adolescent boys and young men about their literacy practices. The authors conclude that while these boys are often skillful readers of "unconventional" texts such as Internet sites, nonfiction, manuals, and magazines, they are not engaged or interested in reading as it is taught in school.

Tovani, Cris. (2000). *I Read It, but I Don't Get It: Comprehension Strategies for Adolescent Readers.* Portland, ME: Stenhouse.

Tovani provides many useful and practical strategies for teaching reading to struggling adolescent readers, including double-entry diaries, "comprehension constructors," and the "coding" or marking of reading problems and relevant corrective strategies.

Trites, Roberta Seelinger. (2000). *Disturbing the Universe: Power and Repression in Adolescent Literature.* Iowa City: University of Iowa Press.

Trites gives a thorough overview of how to understand adolescent or young adult literature through a postmodern lens by analyzing various texts and how they tackle issues of gender, social class, and power/control in modern society. Trites's book is one of the few texts that engage in critical analysis of YA books.

Weaver, Constance. (2002). *Reading Process and Practice.* Portsmouth, NH: Heinemann.

An updated version of the 1988 bestseller, this text offers descriptions of theory and research that can help teachers make appropriate decisions about how to teach reading in secondary schools. It contains definitions of relevant terms as well as practical suggestions for evaluating and instructing students in reading. Weaver gives examples of lessons that could be taught in individual classrooms and also describes what a comprehensive literacy program might look like.

Wilde, Sandra. (2000). *Miscue Analysis Made Easy: Building on Student Strengths.* Portsmouth, NH: Heinemann.

> This is a clear, concise introduction to miscue analysis, namely how and why to do it in your classroom. Wilde includes opportunities to practice marking student readers' miscues and sample forms and templates for teachers to use in conducting their own miscue analyses.

Wilhelm, Jeffrey D. (1997). *"You Gotta BE the Book": Teaching Engaged and Reflective Reading with Adolescents.* New York: Teachers College Press and Urbana, IL: National Council of Teachers of English.

> Wilhelm's premise is that students who have trouble reading have problems visualizing what's going on in the text; therefore, he gives suggestions for helping students visualize textual events through art and dramatic interpretation.

Electronic Resources

ERIC Language Arts Plans
http://askeric.org/Virtual/Lessons/

> This site provides links to many English language arts lesson plans.

The International Reading Association
www.reading.org/

> The homepage of the IRA provides links to conference information, book lists, books you can buy through their publishing house, and information about political and news events affecting literacy instruction in the United States and abroad.

NCTE Notes Plus
www.ncte.org/notesplus/

> This site provides links to classroom ideas about teaching literature, as well as other language and literacy content. It also provides information about how to receive *Classroom Notes Plus*, published by the National Council of Teachers of English.

Young Adult Literature: Middle and Secondary English Language Arts
http://falcon.jmu.edu/~ramseyil/yalit.htm

> This page offers links to multiple projects, guides, and resources about teaching children's, YA, and classic literature.

Your Kids Library
http://yourkidslibrary.com/

> This page includes reviews of every Newbery Medal winner and Honor Book since 1940 as well as ideas for integrating the books into a secondary curriculum.

2 Narratives about Teaching Writing

Most of us have stories to tell about teaching writing or learning to write. Some of our stories describe strong teaching practices that had positive effects; others are horror stories of grammar overkill and five-paragraph essays that were more like fill-in-the-blank assignments than real writing. Often our university teacher education students tell narratives about the killer paper they remember from high school or the time they were allowed to transform their writing project into a dramatic performance. We tend to remember teachers of writing for specific attributes, such as being sticklers for grammar or their affinity for red pen marks that covered our writing. We also hear, on a more uplifting note, about the teachers who encourage students to explore new genres and expand their understanding of audience or who assign journal writing to increase fluency and motivation.

Many of us come to the teaching of writing as successful and motivated former student writers. In high school, Janet wrote religiously in her journal and learned through reflection on her experiences that ungraded journaling could be an important part of her classroom, while Jonathan was a high school journalist, and that experience led to his focus on real audiences and genres in his writing classroom.

One of the challenges for young teachers is to reach out to all students, not just the motivated and excited few who are interested and successful in all writing tasks. This attempt to motivate, this desire to inspire students to be writers, is a continual challenge that affects our daily practice. As teachers of writing, it is up to us to develop our philosophy of the teaching of composition and give our students opportunities to have rich writing experiences. This chapter should help you begin this process.

What Is *Good* Writing Instruction?

Different teachers have different ideas about what constitutes "good" writing pedagogy. Our overriding belief about the teaching of writing is that it should be contextual. That is, we must learn to adapt strategies for specific classroom situations and various audiences. Professional writing, for example, with its emphasis on writing as a means of meeting client needs and problem solving, involves teaching strategies that are different from those for writing about literature. Likewise, the teaching of writing in a middle school is very different from that in a high school setting. Similar arguments could be made for various cultural contexts and socioeconomic situations. We believe, however, that some concepts can guide most writing pedagogy in secondary school classrooms. These are not absolutes, but they can help us as we make decisions about our classrooms and think about the narratives in this chapter.

As in Chapter 1, we challenge you to develop a philosophy of teaching—this time of teaching writing. Why is it important to assign writing in your classes? What kinds of writing should be assigned? What exactly is "process writing," and how can it be incorporated into writing activities? You will begin to explore these questions as you establish a philosophy of writing instruction in the secondary school. To help you begin this exploration, we adapt a list of best practices in writing instruction. In "Best Practice in Writing," a chapter in their influential text *Best Practice: New Standards for Teaching and Learning in America's Schools* (1998), Zemelman, Daniels, and Hyde describe an overview of traits that can be generally considered best practices in writing instruction. The following list of approaches is derived from their overview, with our additions and interpretations. As in Chapter 1, if you wish to read more about any of these approaches, please consult the annotated bibliography at the end of this chapter.

Characteristics of Effective Secondary Writing Pedagogy

1. Adolescents Should Write Often. Communication through language is an inherently human trait; therefore, early forms of writing often occur before formal instruction. Young children "play" at writing as a developmental tool; for example, they produce drawings that have iconographic meanings and often begin writing words using invented spellings. As students reach the middle and high school grades, they often have lost this desire to play with language and write for fun. This tendency toward language play can, however, be unearthed and revitalized by the creative teacher. Many composition theorists and teacher educators advocate frequent writing assignments in secondary schools to report on learning, to facilitate learning processes, and to engage students in creative expression. Janet Emig (1971), for example, differentiates between extensive (school-sponsored) and reflexive (personal, self-sponsored) writing and concludes that high schools are more likely to engage students in extensive writing activities. She urges teachers to include more reflexive assignments in their curricula. James Britton (1975) identifies three different ways of writing: transactional (informative), expressive (personal—also the central mode of written expression for Britton), and poetic (creative, patterned), and he urges secondary teachers to include all three types in their lessons. Such frequent and varied writing can lead to increased fluency, increased mastery of content area skills and knowledge, and eventually increased communicative effectiveness.

2. Teachers Should Encourage Student Ownership of Writing. The ultimate responsibility for writing lies with the writer. Teachers develop frameworks and concepts for writing projects, but they must allow students the freedom to develop ownership of their writing. What exactly does ownership mean, and how does a teacher encourage it in his students? Ownership, by our definition, means something akin to taking responsibility for a writing task or a writer becoming aware of her process so that she can self-evaluate the effectiveness of a piece of writing and revise accordingly, perhaps with the help of outside readers. Ownership of writing can encompass a variety of pedagogical strategies, including giving students choices among writing topics and supplying them with feedback and evaluative response without resorting to overly specific commentary that simply tells students what to change to improve their grade. Nancie Atwell (1998) discusses ownership by students of both their reading and their writing processes and products. She suggests a writing workshop approach in which students are writing on different, self-selected topics yet share similar knowledge about planning, revision, and editing.

Some postmodern or postprocess composition theorists are skeptical of the idea of ownership because of the inherently rhetorical and social nature of the writing act; how can a writer "own" a piece of writing if its very creation is dependent on the cultural and social contexts in which it was written? There is a great deal of truth in this skepticism, and we recognize that a writer does not create a piece of writing in a social or rhetorical vacuum. We believe, however, that the concept of ownership as we define it is a useful one for English teachers seeking to encourage student engagement with and interest in writing. There are many ways to nurture student ownership, and such ownership often leads to increased student motivation, more positive attitudes about writing and the language arts, and increased likelihood that students will effectively complete assignments.

3. Teachers Can Help Students Find Authentic Reasons to Write.
Writing must be treated as a valuable resource, not only in school but
also in the wider social and professional world in which students will
live and work as adults. Topics should be as meaningful for students
as possible; in- or out-of-class publishing and the inclusion of real audiences in writing assignments are among the strongest motivators for
student writing. Contemporary cultural studies approaches to writing
instruction often include discussion of service-learning programs that
require students to engage in volunteer or out-of-class work with local
social service agencies and then write about some aspect of their experience. While this approach may not be feasible at the middle or high
school level, teachers *can* ask students to research and write about topics of interest or concern in their local communities and schools instead
of the distant and archaic topics students are often asked to write about.
Teachers can also approach the teaching of writing from a rhetorical
perspective, taking into consideration issues of audience, purpose, and
effect.

Other ways to bring the real world into the writing classroom and
create authentic writing experiences for students include inviting professional writers to class as guest speakers or having students share their
texts with people outside of the school and ask for their feedback or
response. Many teachers already do quite a bit of in-class (or even in-
school) publication, such as posting papers on a bulletin board or publishing them in a school newspaper or literary magazine. All of these
are ideas that can provide an audience for student writing that is larger
and more "real" than the sole audience of the teacher-grader. As a result, students may (1) try harder, (2) place more value on writing, and
(3) understand writing as a part of professional and adult life.

**4. Effective Writing Assignments Involve the Complete Writing Pro-
cess.** Writing should be valued as an ongoing process; value should be
placed on writing as a process of inquiry, in addition to a final tangible
product. In the 1970s and '80s, process writing was introduced to secondary English teachers by such theorists and educators as Peter Elbow
(1973), Donald Murray (1968), and Ken Macrorie (1976). While the ideas
of these pedagogues are still alive in current composition studies, they
have been expanded by the social constructivist and postprocess theories of others such as James Berlin (1988, 1996), John Trimbur (1989), and
Patricia Bizzell (1992) who have added a contextual component to the
writing process, a component that takes into consideration the social
and material realities of the writer, the time and place of the writing act,

and the ideologies often at play when a writer tackles a communicative task.

The writing process is generally known to encompass five stages that are viewed as recursive and sometimes simultaneous: planning, prewriting, drafting, revision, and editing. These recursive steps and the opportunity for students to engage in them should be included in most writing assignments or instructional units. Planning involves thinking about a piece of writing and deciding on a general direction or topic; prewriting activities include outlining, mapping, drawing, clustering, freewriting, listing, and other tasks that facilitate or reflect thinking; drafting is the writer's first best attempt at writing down ideas; revision involves making changes in word choice, sentence structure, organization, or content/details included; and editing is proofreading or correcting errors in grammar, usage, and punctuation. Students can engage in a type of revision called "reformulation," or "deep" revision. Reformulation requires making major changes to the structure of a piece of writing, not simply changes to surface features. Examples include selecting a different point of view, tone, thematic focus, or audience.

5. Teachers Can Help Students Get Started. An important role of teachers in the writing process occurs early on, in the planning and prewriting stages. Teachers should encourage and guide students as they generate ideas. Also, skillful teachers help student writers gather and organize materials that facilitate the planning of their writing project. How can teachers go about providing this support for student writers? In the rest of this chapter, some specific ideas are presented through the narratives, but in general, teachers can provide classroom time and opportunity for students to think through ideas and/or generate writing topics. One-on-one conferencing, peer group conferencing, and teacher-led whole-group practice in prewriting are all possible ways of supporting the early stages of students' writing processes.

6. Teachers Can Help Students Draft and Revise. In a similar spirit to the previous point, teachers can also provide valuable assistance (through one-on-one interaction and through effective pedagogical strategies) during the drafting and revision processes. We know that good writing comes through repeated drafting, revision, and reenvisioning of ideas. A teacher's goal is to guide students though a writing process and then, with practice and feedback, help them to internalize their own process so that they can continue to apply it in later writing tasks throughout their academic and professional lives. This help can occur through conferencing, establishment of peer workshopping groups, commentary on student texts, and whole-class practice of various writing strategies.

7. Grammar and Mechanics Are Learned in the Context of Actual Writing. Grammar, usage, and punctuation should not be taught in ways that are decontextualized or separated from actual writing projects, such as through handbook drills. Many educational researchers and theorists have reached this conclusion, as early as 1906 and continuing to the present day. While a few research studies defend the study of formal grammar more or less in isolation (Neuleib, 1977; Kolln, 1981; Holt, 1982), they are outnumbered by the multitude of studies that advocate a contextualized approach to grammar instruction that teaches grammar, usage, and other stylistic issues while students are engaged in the writing process and at a point when these concepts and skills are relevant. Instead of teaching traditional or formal grammatical terminology to improve writing quality, we believe that extensive writing practice, along with consistent and relevant feedback, helps to produce fluent writing and accurate and effective grammar usage. Additionally, grammar should be integrated into the later stages of the writing process (e.g., editing) and be deemphasized in the planning, prewriting, and drafting phases so that these relatively lower-order concerns are not privileged over the exploration and development of ideas. For continued, in-depth discussion of teaching grammar and language, see Chapter 3.

8. Teachers Can Create a Classroom Writing Community. We have already mentioned publication (both in the classroom and in the wider community) as an important part of the writing process because it helps create authentic audiences. Another reason to publish student work within the classroom is that it has a community-building effect. Sharing writing through bulletin board postings, weekly "author's chair" celebrations (Atwell, 1998), and class publications provides opportunities for classroom talk, peer-to-peer feedback, and, when publication is done within a positive context, the development of feelings of safety and an increased tendency to take academic and intellectual risks. While possibly no classroom will ever succeed in being a risk-free space, especially when grades have to be given, a teacher can create an instructional space in which students recognize that writing is a process during which they are expected to engage in inquiry and exploration and that this process does not always result in the most effective pieces of writing the first time around. Such a space can foster a collaborative, workshoplike environment instead of a competitive one in which students compete for the best grade and desperately seek to discover "what the teacher wants."

9. Writing Should Extend throughout the Curriculum. Writing is one of the best tools for learning in many disciplines; therefore, writing can and should be incorporated in math, science, social studies, health, and any other subject area, both while students are learning new material and while they are reporting on what has been learned. Writing To Learn, Writing Across the Disciplines (WID), and Writing Across the Curriculum (WAC) programs have demonstrated these benefits of the writing process (Fulwiler & Young, 1990). English language arts teachers, by the nature of their professional expertise, may be called upon in their schools to mentor content area teachers who wish to incorporate more writing into their classes. We should relish and take full advantage of these opportunities to share our knowledge of the writing process and its connection to learning and cognitive, social, and emotional development.

10. Teachers Can Use Evaluation Constructively and Efficiently. Too many red marks can be counterproductive, both for the student writer who is tentative about the quality of his or her other skills and the teacher with 120 students a day and a limited amount of time for evaluating student writing. Instead of meticulous and extensive commenting to justify final grades, writing should be evaluated in terms of process with the goal of improvement, not judgment, in mind. This type of evaluation might include in-process student-teacher conferences, portfolio systems, "minimal marking" approaches that use a coding system such as checkmarks in the margins of papers to indicate errors (Haswell, 1983), grading only selected pieces, and peer or self-evaluation. Many contemporary compositionists support this view, stressing that overcommenting and a focus on evaluation instead of feedback or response can have a negative effect on students' writing quality and their attitudes toward writing. There is a difference between providing feedback or commentary on student writing and assigning it a letter or numerical grade. While grading, like it or not, is required in most U.S. secondary schools, we can learn to be more effective when evaluating by accompanying grades with complementary response and using rubrics or scoring guides. When possible, evaluation should be more formative (during the process of writing) than summative (after the writing is complete) and more constructive than punitive.

Teachers should remember that grading has a political aspect in addition to a practical one. Grades, or "terminal evaluation" (Murray,

1968), often reflect or enforce hierarchal relationships between students and teachers and can lead to a decrease in student confidence about writing if used in a punitive fashion.

Controversies in Writing Instruction

The characteristics of best practice in writing are not prescriptive; instead, they constitute an array of choices from which we can select based on our students' needs. Within writing pedagogy, however, there are controversies that reoccur in discussions among English teachers and composition theorists. Not everyone shares the same views or defines best practice in the same way. Following are descriptions of some of the controversies that we have heard the most about in recent years.

1. **Nonacademic Writing versus Academic Writing.** Best practice tells us that we should help students find "real" reasons to write. But what are the parameters of this writing? Some theorists tell us that the only way to write in the English language arts classroom is by using academic genres (research essays, literary essays, and so forth), while others take a different perspective, encouraging students to write for what they call "authentic" audiences (research reports to local politicians, book reviews to be published in local newspapers, or memoirs written for family members). Advocates of academic writing seem to believe that secondary school writing is primarily a preparation for college-level writing, and students must learn how to write in academic genres in order to succeed at the next level. Proponents of writing for "real audiences" tend to be those with more of a writing-across-the-curriculum bent who believe that actual writing tasks have a more practical or rhetorical aspect; that is, writers write with a particular audience and purpose in mind, and an academic audience is not the one most students will be writing for in their adult lives. They argue that writing should prepare students for professional life and the writing tasks they will complete on the job as adults.

2. **Evaluation and Response.** Some English teachers see the final product as the ultimate goal of writing instruction and grade solely on final drafts and other final products. Others, however, put minimal emphasis on final work and develop systems of grading such as portfolios and scoring rubrics that emphasize work that leads up to the final product (drafts, prewriting, research activities, peer workshop group participation, and the quality of response to peers). Some see peer response groups as a way to polish final products and take care of minor editing

concerns, while others see collaborative groups as places to work on higher-order concerns (such as organization, development, and other large-scale issues) and prefer to leave the lower-order issues (spelling, grammar) for a later time. We think there should be a way to strike a compromise between these philosophical binaries.

Sometimes unconventional grading is equated with lax or minimal standards, and teachers who give primarily high grades (or who choose not to grade some student work) are seen as too "easy." This linkage of traditional number or letter grades with high standards (and therefore student learning) is at the heart of this debate as administrators at both secondary and college levels voice concern over what they call "grade inflation" and the supposed negative effect it is having on student learning. Proponents of alternative grading practices, such as portfolios, argue that higher grades do not mean lower standards but instead often mean that students are achieving at higher levels because of improved pedagogical practices often directly linked to assessment strategies.

3. The Great Grammar Debate. The concept of Standard English is one near and dear to the hearts of many English teachers dedicated to the teaching of traditional grammar, usage, and mechanics. Standard English can be defined as that which is grammatically and mechanically "correct" according to handbooks and grammar textbooks. It is important, however, to remember that Standard English is spoken primarily by those with political, social, and economic power, and consequently our students' speech often does not take this form. So what do we do? Do we give up the teaching of Standard English in favor of allowing students to write and speak in their own home dialects? This has been a debate in recent years partially because of the relationship between dialectical difference and race, ethnicity, or social class. If we believe that writing is based on the specific needs of the audience, then how can we tell whether the dialect or style being used is appropriate? And the bigger question: how do we succeed both in providing students with knowledge that will enable them to interact in professional contexts in which Standard English is required and in reassuring them that their home dialects are valued and important? Some colleagues ask students to write "memos" that accompany final written products explaining how the text meets the needs of the audience and hence explaining the use of dialects other than Standard English. Other teachers engage their students in discussions of Standard English and the sociopolitical contexts in which it might be privileged and the reasons for this privileging. In this way, Standard English is addressed as an ideological expression of social and economic class—not just as a set of rules to be remembered and enacted.

Narratives

Here we present four stories that focus on the teaching of writing by teachers of middle or high school English. We chose these narratives to represent the range of issues and situations that occur in a writing classroom. These narratives, and the subsequent responses from experienced teachers or teacher educators, should be used as opportunities to reflect on and discuss what it means to be a teacher of writing. As in the previous chapter, the responses are not prescriptive; instead, they are included to open up discussion and help readers develop their own theories about teaching writing.

The first story, "Why Won't He Write?," is concerned with one of the most common problems we encounter: encouraging a reluctant student to write creatively and join the classroom writing community. Do we push him and risk alienating him for the rest of the school year? Or do we "let him slide," with the opposite danger of not helping him learn to write? The second narrative, "The Rite of Passage: Writing the Research Paper," discusses a reluctant student working on a research project as his teacher seeks better ways to plan her writing assignment in order to increase his motivation and confidence. The third story, "Buried under the Paper Load," discusses another common classroom concern: how does a teacher effectively respond to writing assignments when he or she might see more than 120 students each day? The fourth and last narrative, "Reviewing Peer Review," tells the story of a teacher implementing peer review in her high school classroom and wondering how she can make the technique effective for all of her student writers.

Writing Narrative 1

Motivating students to write is one of the greatest challenges for English teachers. Here is one story about such a struggle that raises questions about approaching resistant writers. How can we set up our classrooms to inspire students to write? How can we overcome student apathy about writing? How can we urge students to join a classroom writing community? This story takes place in a small, rural high school in central Missouri where DJ is a senior in a creative writing class.

Why Won't He Write?

DJ would come to my creative writing class every day with no books, no paper, and no pencil. He would sort of slink into the room and slide into his desk a full two minutes before the bell rang. But he would be carrying nothing; his hands might be shoved into the pockets of his green plastic jacket. DJ was what you might call a reluctant writer. He seemed unable to sustain any independent fluent writing for more than a minute. Religiously, he would opt to go into the computer lab (which was next door to my classroom) to draft his papers, poems, and stories; however, few actual words would emerge on the screen. Instead, he would type a couple of words while I was looking over his shoulder, but as soon as my back was turned he would execute one or two computer clicks and be on the Internet or in a taboo chat room. Sometimes he would just sit and change the font and size of what he had written countless times until class was over. DJ was computer savvy, so he loved to sit in front of the screen and play. And, paradoxically, DJ loved to read and would often talk about long sci fi novels he was currently engaged in. But writing? That was a different story for DJ. Consequently, he was quiet in class, well behaved, and appeared to be on task, but rarely ever was. Sometimes it was easy to forget about DJ because outwardly he demanded little attention. In fact, he seemed to prefer being left alone.

This day is no different. We are working on a final draft of a Halloween story, a scary narrative that students usually love to sink their teeth into. Even though most of the class is in the revision or editing stage, DJ has yet to draft anything. Whenever I can find time, I work one-on-one with DJ (there are twenty-five other students in the class demanding my attention), trying to help him generate ideas. But I have had little success, as usual.

I walk over to DJ and sit down beside him. He sits transfixed in front of his Macintosh computer, staring at the displayed data, which I have no idea how he has accessed or even what it is. I ask him to show me what he has written, and he clicks back to the proper document. All he has written is "**A DARK NIGHT**," but it is beautifully centered across the top of the blank page.

"That's a great title. Where do you plan to go from here?"

"I don't know."

"Well, what might be the setting of this scary story? Who might a character be?"

"I don't know." He performs a click with the mouse, eyes fixed on the screen. He opens the control panel and tinkers with the volume level.

"Tell me a scary story that you've heard before."

"Well, there was the one about the man with the hook for a hand and the two kids in the car." Click, again. **DARK NIGHT** changes into a symbolic pattern, ΔAPK NIΓHT. Click, and it morphs into a delicate script, *DARK NIGHT.*

"Okay. Is there any way you can modify that idea into a story of your own? Use it as a basis for your own story?"

"I could have the man with the hook be a vampire."

"Okay. Go with that. Let's write that down."

With a sigh, DJ clicks back on his blank page and writes underneath DARK NIGHT, "There was a vampire with a hooked hand. On a dark night he found two teenagers . . ."

He seems to be on a roll.

"Good. Keep going." Another student calls for me. I move away to help Amy with her story about a depressed werewolf. Five minutes later I look toward DJ's computer. He's in a chat room for *Star Wars* fans. I know he still doesn't have a draft, and the final story is due tomorrow. He'll fail yet another assignment. How in the world do I work successfully with DJ?

A Teacher Responds

This is a situation that I think every English teacher has been in at one time or another. Sometimes, despite what seem to be our best efforts, some students, for whatever reason, tend to resist whatever we are doing. I am going to offer some suggestions for the teacher, but first I want to discuss something not to do: become frustrated or angry. One of the initial reactions of novice teachers (and some experienced ones, too) is to turn the students' lack of work into a personal matter ("I put together this great assignment and all he wants to do is go into a chat room. I would have *loved* this assignment when I was in high school!"). Resist this impulse!

After class, take a step back and then begin to consider the situation and look at some options. Talk to other teachers who know DJ; consult an English teacher listserv, Web site, or journal for ideas, and then begin to think about what to do next. This inquiry-based, reflexive approach to teaching encourages the teacher to analyze the pedagogical problem instead of allowing emotion and frustration to guide decision making.

In this case, it looks to me as if DJ is having trouble getting started. Beginning a writing task, whether a story, essay, poem, or anything else, can be intimidating and frustrating. When I cannot start a piece of writing, I also tend to procrastinate, surfing Web sites or checking e-mail. I suspect this may be the case with DJ as well. It may be that the teacher has not provided enough support for the writing task or given opportunities for planning and prewriting activities. In an attempt to develop creativity, the teacher may not have provided enough guidance to the students concerning the writing assignment and the nature of the writing process (e.g., setting parameters, teaching the desired genre, developing and supporting prewriting and drafting exercises).

Although there might be other outside-of-the-classroom issues to deal with as well, I would recommend as a first step talking to DJ to find out why he is having trouble starting his story. Chances are he will say that he "has nothing to write about." So I would give him some heuristics (e.g., story starters or prewriting strategies) as ways to think of ideas and supply him with strategies to help him develop some essential elements of his story to ease in his drafting. These strategies could include prewriting exercises such as listing or clustering in which he describes the setting and characters or visually maps a plot. From this point on, peer groups could be used to help DJ move from planning and prewriting to drafting and revision. These peer groups could provide oral and written response, in addition to the teacher's response, on the developing draft. In this way, DJ begins to be acclimated to the classroom writing community; he engages in writing conversations with his peers and begins to feel like a fellow author. Perhaps he will begin to feel some ownership over his writing task instead of seeing it simply as something he is doing to satisfy the whims of his teacher.

Another point that should be made is that the narrative doesn't explain what the nature of the initial assignment was. Did the teacher hand out an assignment sheet? If so, what did it say? If not, how was the assignment given? If the assignment was not given in a specific or detailed way, the teacher might consider crafting future assignments more carefully, taking into consideration planning, prewriting, and audience. With some modifications in pedagogical approach, the quality of DJ's writing, as well as his attitude toward it, could be much improved.

A Teacher Responds

DJ reminds me of students I have struggled with over the years. Reluctant writers exist in our classes at all levels and across all content areas. Unfortunately, there isn't a guaranteed recipe for helping them engage—at least I haven't found one. What I have found, however, is that students who exhibit reluctance similar to DJ's often do so because of their previous (and maybe current) experiences with writing. Finding out about these experiences and the pre(mis)conceptions that a student writer brings with him or her is usually a good place to start with resistant writers.

From the narrative, we might assume that DJ enjoys reading and understands the relationship between a reader and the written word. Unlike many of our reluctant writers, his resistance does not seem rooted in limited reading skills or a negative attitude toward reading. I wouldn't rule these out, however, since the narrative doesn't tell us much about DJ's reading habits except that he loves to read and talk about science fiction novels. Learning more about his reading strategies and interests and about the ways in which he talks about whatever he reads could provide insight into his attitudes toward, experiences with, and habits in writing. I would like to know more about how DJ connects reading and writing. What relationships does he see between the processes? Why does he seem to retreat from writing yet engage with reading? Most teachers gather this information over time as they converse with students, listen to comments in class discussions, and observe behaviors in class. DJ's teacher might want to conduct a more deliberate interview with him to learn more about the attitudes and expectations he brings with him into the writing class. The teacher might want to learn more about DJ's digital reading and writing experiences as well, since DJ seems to choose these when given the opportunity. What intrigues him about surfing and participating in chat rooms? How actively engaged is he? What reading and writing does he choose to do when he surfs and chats?

In their studies of adolescent boys, Michael Smith and Jeffrey Wilhelm (2002) found that many high school boys feel that the use of electronic technologies provides them more control and possibility than they are given in typical school situations. The use of computers allows them choice and therefore a sense of competence. We don't know enough about DJ from the narrative to know if his playing around on the computer provides the efficacy that he misses elsewhere, but this line of inquiry might help the teacher decide how to approach the next writing assignment. Giving students more choice in both the topics they investigate and the genres they select could be a strategy that would engage DJ.

Like many teachers, DJ's writing teacher might design the students' writing assignments to meet curricular requirements. Offering students writing opportunities in which they select the topics they write about, the purposes and audiences for their writings, and the genres they believe are appropriate is difficult for many teachers to handle due both to the pressures they feel to "cover" requirements and to the management issues involved in such differentiation. DJ could be a student who needs such openness in order to engage, however. This does not mean he will not need a teacher's support once he begins. Scaffolding is defined as providing instruction that helps students make connections between prior knowledge or interests and new information or expectations. Scaffolding writing instruction in a classroom in which each student is at a different stage in the process, is writing in different genres for different purposes, and is grappling with different writing problems can be a logistical nightmare for a teacher. Yet it can also be one of the most authentic and exciting environments for everyone involved in the classroom writing community if students are encouraged to collaborate and support one another. DJ's teacher might want to explore writing workshop approaches and investigate how other writing teachers provide guidance to students within differentiated classrooms. The teacher also might explore how to use writing portfolios as a vehicle for offering students authentic choices while holding them accountable for the specified writing standards of the curriculum.

Until we know a little more about DJ's skills and attitudes—his previous experiences with writing instruction in school, his current interests and habits in reading and writing both in and outside of school, his preconceptions about the processes involved in writing and about his own abilities—we won't know if he needs more support (i.e., conferencing, questioning, brainstorming, mapping) in getting started with the writing task given to him or if he needs more choice and freedom in developing writing tasks that are meaningful to him. Writing scary stories is often an engaging activity for adolescent writers, so DJ's teacher has not necessarily chosen unwisely for the assignment, but the teacher has been the one doing the choosing. This fact alone may serve to disengage a student writer who could become an eager participant in the classroom community if supported by the teacher in *designing* as well as completing writing experiences.

Choice and authenticity are two of twelve standards for effective learning that Phillip Schlechty (2002) recommends for overall school improvement. He describes how students respond to school tasks using five categories: authentic engagement, ritual engagement, passive compliance, retreatism, and rebellion. DJ's behaviors in the preceding narrative are similar to Schlechty's description of retreatism:

> [T]he task has no attraction to the student, and the student is not compelled by other considerations to do anything active to support the task. The student simply withdraws—mentally and sometimes physically—from what is going on in the immediate environment. (p. 11)

DJ's teacher may want to investigate what researchers are learning about the roles of choice and ownership in engaged learning. Like Schlechty, Harvey Daniels and Marilyn Bizar (1998) identify student choice as one of the "vital ingredients" necessary for genuine learning. Their suggestions for conferencing, forming classroom workshops, and embedding self-assessment into the daily routines of the class might offer a useful starting point for the teacher's investigation.

For Further Discussion

1. What are some prewriting strategies that can be introduced to students? How do teachers know which ones are most appropriate? Which ones do you think might work most effectively with DJ? Thinking back to your middle and high school years, which ones do you think would have worked best for you?

2. What is your opinion of the teacher's response to DJ's lack of motivation? Do you think a more structured creative writing assignment, as the first respondent suggests, would detract from the freedom necessary for students to write creatively? Why or why not?

3. Hypothesize about the connections between reading and writing. Do you think a richer understanding of DJ's reading habits could help the teacher encourage him to write? If so, how?

Learning Activities

1. Practice some prewriting activities the next time you write a paper: clustering or mapping, freewriting, listing, or outlining. Reflect on how useful they are for you. Then think about how you might implement such activities in a creative writing assignment for students.

2. Taking into consideration what you know about DJ, develop a writing assignment that you think he would enjoy.

Writing Narrative 2

Research writing is an important part of many English classrooms. Many teachers, however, accept the lockstep notions of the research process: note cards, bibliography cards, outlines, etc. But there are many ways to achieve the goals of a research project through more interesting and relevant means. Teachers could, for example, use alternative genres such as PowerPoint presentations and Web sites, or they could use a version of Ken Macrorie's (1988) "I-Search" paper for which students develop real questions of interest to them and explore possible answers. In this case, we see a teacher struggle to engage a student in a traditional research process. What could she have done to make the project more meaningful? How could she have facilitated his writing process? This narrative takes place in a small high school in rural Virginia.

The Rite of Passage: Writing the Research Paper

The senior year research paper. A rite of passage. You could recite the assignment in your sleep: Choose a topic on which reasonable people could disagree. Explain the issue, discuss various perspectives, and then offer your own thoughtful opinion. Like those before them, my students would soon be able to reminisce about index cards, citing, bibliographies, footnotes, and endnotes. It was going well: students were writing about issues of gun control, euthanasia, abortion, even the environmental issues concerning stream management for livestock farmers.

Then there was Jason. He had taken to sitting in the far left corner, alone, with his head propped up against the cinder block wall. His six-foot frame stuck out at awkward angles. He talked to no one and either slept or made snide comments under his breath. He was beginning to unnerve me.

But he hadn't always been that way. I remember seeing him during his junior year, often in conversation with his English or shop teacher before and after class. And in the beginning of this year, he had participated a lot, challenging ideas and thinking out loud. But by April, he had become sullen and his participation had waned. He had stopped handing in work, he rarely passed a test, and his grades were barely scraping by.

So when topics for the research paper were due, I wasn't surprised that Jason didn't have one. When the first round of research cards was due and Jason didn't have any, I was frustrated. It wasn't that he *couldn't* do it; he was just flat out refusing. As the students filed out one Friday afternoon, I caught his attention: "Jason, what's up? I'm not getting anything from you."

"I know, I know." He extracted himself from the current of kids. "There's nothing to do. It's all so boring."

"Well, let's think. What are you interested in? This is a big part of your quarter grade. What are you really interested in?" I wanted to reach him, find a connection and bring him back.

He dropped his head back in bored exasperation; "I'll have something Monday, okay? Can I go now?"

Monday before school, he poked his head in my room.

"Ms. S., look." He looked pleased, and I felt myself get excited.

"Whatcha got?"

"Well, I want to do mine on the *Titanic.* It is so cool. I'm really into it as a ship, and just how it was so big. Just everything, I think it's cool." He had handwritten two pages in careful cursive, all about the *Titanic* (understand this happened well before Leonardo DiCaprio). As the words tumbled out of his mouth, I felt my insides tighten.

"Jason, that is cool. But what *about* the *Titanic?* The research paper has to deal with an issue."

A heavy silence. " I don't know. I just . . . this is what I want to do."

The shuffling and morning chaos was getting louder outside my door. I could see my journalism kids pressing to get in. And then I turned back to Jason, leaned in, and tried to find a connection.

"Well, is there an issue about the *Titanic?* Something that would allow you to research the different arguments and then say what you think?"

He exploded: "You say you want me to do something I want to do and so I find something and now you say no!"

"I'm not saying no, Jason, what I am saying is there needs to be an issue, something that there are at least two sides to."

"This is bullshit," and he walked out, pushing his way through the kids in the hall.

Later, when we met in class, I approached him. I was firm but not cold. I repeated the guidelines for the research paper, gave him deadlines, which would catch him up, and told him I was available

▶

if he wanted to conference about the paper. He said nothing in return and maintained his silence the rest of the year. He never did the research paper and failed the quarter.

A Teacher Responds

The research paper is the perennial "thorn in the side" of English teachers. Our curricula often require it, administrators and parents expect it, and we even see the value in such a project. But we cannot figure out how to convince students of its value. Even if students find topics they like, such as Jason and the *Titanic*, we have to push hard to get them to produce anything but a book report linking bits of information gleaned from library reference books. And then, if we throw in the bit about quoting versus paraphrasing (along with a dash of plagiarism paranoia), how to do a works cited page, and the proper way to write a note card, we lose our students altogether. Not only are they frustrated—they are bored.

So what might this teacher have done to motivate Jason? She could have allowed him to write the paper as he desired, and she probably would have received the aforementioned book report. Or she might have revisited her initial assignment and rethought how she presented the research paper to her students. Allowing Jason to spend more time prewriting and producing early rough drafts could have helped him focus his paper. Often students figure out what they really want to write through actually writing, but this discovery is dependent on being given the time to freewrite, create graphic organizers, and talk with peers. This teacher might also have considered encouraging her students to write about issues that have more immediate relevance in their lives and communities. Instead of writing about the *Titanic*, for example, Jason might have opted to explore whether success in high school athletics correlates with success in college athletics. With such topics, students might sustain their motivation longer for the project and with less prodding from their teachers.

Another path the teacher might have considered is structuring the research assignment similar to Ken Macrorie's "I-Search" paper (1988). The I-Search assignment asks students to begin not with a topic but with a question they are genuinely interested in answering. Instead of being purely expository, the paper becomes more argumentative as students explore this question. They are not simply providing information about a topic; they are explaining why something is or is not a certain way. This focus on exploring a question provides a built-in thesis statement when students attempt to answer it. In Jason's case, for example, instead of choosing the general topic of the *Titanic* he might have identified the question, "Why did the *Titanic* sink?" Or "Who survived the *Titanic* and why?" Consequently, his research path would have been more focused and potentially more thoughtful and satisfying as he conducted research in order to answer his question and report his findings to others.

A Teacher Responds

The problem in this scenario is essentially a power struggle. Jason seems to be a disaffected, unengaged student in conflict with the teacher who has aligned her goals specifically, and inflexibly, to the standards set by the curriculum. To diffuse this situation and ensure that Jason achieves some level of success, the teacher should contemplate the specific curricular goals in teaching the research paper and consider some alternate ways to achieve them in her students' best interest. The students should have a sense of ownership in the development of their individual projects. Most important, Jason should have the opportunity to develop and refine his own voice in writing.

On reading this narrative, I was immediately transported back to my English classroom in Michigan, with twenty-five juniors staring blankly at me as I introduced the obligatory research paper in much the same way this teacher did. And there were always three or four Jasons sullenly resisting, questioning, and grumbling as I tried to cajole them into a state of even feigned interest in a topic suitable for outlining, note carding, footnoting, and writing.

Finally, I couldn't take it. I spent a weekend reviewing the curricular guide, contemplating the goals for teaching the research paper. I thought about what I really wanted for my students. Did I want them to find out about something in which they were interested? Did I want them to learn about the finer points of research paper mechanics? Did I want them to learn how to critically evaluate sources? Then it dawned on me that I was thinking only about what *I* wanted, not what *they* wanted. Why shouldn't I ask them? The next day in class we negotiated our goals for the project, and I spent five weeks learning *with* my students. In the end, the results far exceeded not only the expectations for papers I had received in past years but also the expectations we had set together in class.

Teaching "the research paper" is required of nearly every secondary English department. But often the research paper is also taught in another content area, or retaught in college, with different research and documentation criteria. Minutia of documentation and citation vary;

students learn early to make sure they produce what the teacher wants. Consequently, a teacher should think carefully about the goals of a research project within the context of this larger paradigm. Can these goals be achieved in ways that allow more student choice and creativity than the traditional "pick a topic from the list" research paper? Can a student, for example, fulfill the requirements of a research unit through multigenre projects, as outlined in Tom Romano's *Blending Genre, Altering Style: Writing Multigenre Papers* (2000)? Are there interdisciplinary or service-learning opportunities that might lend themselves to the research project? Embedding the research in reality or riding on the coattails of another content area can ratchet up the interest level for an adolescent learner.

Perhaps we have an obligation to teach the research paper, but our obligation is also to differentiate instruction to reach all kinds of learners. When I invited my students to help establish the goals for our research unit, it became clear to me that the larger context of educating young people should not be subsumed into the short-term context of teaching note cards, bib cards, and works cited pages.

One of the most striking moments in this narrative is Jason's attempt to share his ideas with the teacher. His interest in initiating the conference indicates that he is concerned about his progress and desires some level of success with the project. He is still in the discovery phase of writing and should be encouraged with affirming comments such as, "Wow, Jason, you've really thought about this!" followed by genuine questions on the teacher's part ("Why did the *Titanic* sink? How did people react when they heard the news? Did they try to blame someone? Do you think someone was at fault?") to help focus his interest without seeming judgmental. But the teacher, who was concerned about the students in the hallway, retreated to the "verbal red pen" of reiterated assignment guidelines, which limited Jason's options for developing a clear topic and silenced his voice for the project.

Tom Romano in *Clearing the Way* (1987) and Nancie Atwell in *In the Middle* (1998) advocate discovery writing conferences in which the students do most of the talking. The teacher's role is to listen and affirm the student's exploratory thinking, perhaps jotting down ideas the student expresses verbally that may not have made it into the piece of writing just yet. The teacher in this narrative could have taken the time to listen carefully to Jason during the informal conference, and then asked questions rather than passing judgment. Questioning shows the teacher's interest in both the student and the piece of writing he or she produced and also serves as a model for the inquisitive behavior educators hope students will exhibit during a research project. This teacher should have let the journalism kids stand out in the hall for a minute and focused on Jason's attempt to finally make a connection. Taking just a few minutes to listen, engage in dialogue, jot down notes and phrases from the conversation on a sticky note, and give these thoughts to Jason would show him that his ideas are important, even if it means saying, "Jason, can you wait just a minute while I tell these journalism students to chill out there until I open the door?" And, in the end, even if Jason's research paper wasn't perfect, at least it would have been something. Is failing better than a C? Why should Jason be discouraged to the point of failure right from the start?

The next day in class the teacher's "firm but not cold" reiteration to Jason of research paper guidelines clearly shows that there is no negotiation of power in this situation. She has control and Jason's only options are either to conform or to further rebel and fail to complete the requirements for passing the marking period. But Jason already knows the guidelines and has already made his choice. Jason just wants his voice to be heard.

For Further Discussion

1. How would you have responded to Jason's sudden interest in the *Titanic?* What might you have done to help him pursue the project and maintain his enthusiasm? Would you be willing to modify the assignment so that Jason would still do a research project but perhaps one slightly different from the one the rest of the class is doing? Do you think this would compromise the project's integrity, or do you think the benefits to Jason would outweigh any problems?

2. What do you see as the goal of a high school research paper requirement? Why would a teacher include one in her curriculum? What do you think a student should learn as a result of such a project? In a small group, brainstorm reasons for assigning a research paper. Which seem most important? Least?

3. Think about the role of power and authority in the secondary English class. What kind of power or authority should a teacher hold? What types of power or authority should students be allowed to exhibit? Are there certain pedagogical contexts in which power and authority are more important or problematic? Why or why not?

Learning Activities

1. Thinking about your own experiences of writing research papers in middle or high school, devise an assignment sheet for

a research paper project. Building on your discussion of goals (see item 2 above), how would you guide students through the research process? What guidelines would you set for their final papers? Rubrics are lists of criteria that the teacher will evaluate when assessing a paper, as well as the number of points or percentages of value placed on each characteristic. Rubrics can be holistic, requiring teachers to assign one number or point value to a paper after reading the entire piece; analytical, breaking down the characteristics of the paper into various statements that describe necessary qualities (e.g., under "organization" a teacher might include such items has "has strong thesis statement, contains topic sentences, or uses adequate transitions"); or checklists that simply note if various tasks were completed. Create an assignment sheet and a rubric or scoring guide for the paper that shows how you would evaluate students' work.

2. What alternatives can you think of for the traditional research paper? Make a list of different possibilities. These could include performance-based projects, visual projects, art projects, etc.

Writing Narrative 3

Most teachers hate to grade. The idea of putting scores on what we see as creative works can be very disconcerting—and time consuming. But grading is a necessity and unavoidable for most English language arts teachers. Many alternatives for grading exist, however, including process-oriented grading such as portfolios, and rubrics or scoring guides can make our task easier and evaluation more useful for students. In this story, we see a teacher who avoids grading and tries to focus on "bigger issues." But in doing so, he sets himself up for some end-of-term difficulties. How can we strike a balance between graded and nongraded work? Which things should we grade? Which should we simply respond to? This story takes place in a midsize suburban high school in the upper Midwest.

Buried under the Paper Load

I remember my first year as a teacher. I was teaching ninth-grade English and loving it. My students were fun and full of life. I was teaching literature and writing that I enjoyed. My principal and department heads were both supportive and committed. It just seemed too good to be true. And then it happened. I guess I shouldn't describe it like that, as if it came upon me all of a sudden. It was more like a slow, suffocating death grip than a surprise. What I'm referring to, of course, is grading. The *G* word. As the first quarter came to a close, I looked at the "writing" portion of my grade book (a standard part of my school's "language arts/English" block grade system) and realized that I had little numerically to show for all the work my students had done. I couldn't give or justify grades for many of their assignments. Instead, all I had in the little green boxes were some checkmarks to show that things had been turned in. I knew I would be in trouble if someone questioned me on my grading scheme. The truth was, I didn't really have a scheme. I started having nightmares about parents storming into my room waving unsatisfactory grade cards. The district grade sheet with its little bubbles to be filled in taunted me. I knew I had to do some grading.

I had boxes of dialogic journals and piles of ungraded poetry portfolios and essays that I had started to evaluate but stopped reading when I became frustrated with my arbitrary attempts to select a grade. How did I know if the work was an A or a B? The student had worked really hard on this one, so did that justify an A even if the quality was more of a B? What are an A and a B anyway? Sheesh. It seemed to me that the real work had already been done. The students had completed the assignments and learned from them. Why must I rank them? But despite my internal, philosophical aversion to grading, I knew I had to do it. The grade sheets had arrived in my mailbox, and they had to be completed and returned in one week. What was I to do? Give everyone an A? Give half the class As and half Bs? Quit my job and move to Cuba?

Well, I decided that none of those options would do, so I looked at the assignments my students had completed the first nine weeks. Students had written daily journals and kept literature response journals. They had also created poetry portfolios that included poems they liked and essays in response to these poems. I was thrilled with the progress of my students and the quality of their work. But I was flustered when it came to evaluating this work. The amount of paperwork was killing me. I had already spent hours responding to journals after school and reading some wonderful comments and discussions, but I wondered if students read my responses. But what if I didn't respond? Would they think I didn't care? Would they understand the importance of writing as a means of expression and thinking? And in addition, these responses I spent so many hours crafting didn't provide what I now needed: numbers or letters to put on the grade report sheet. When students finished a writing project, I could respond, but when it came to evaluation, I was paralyzed. How could I grade a creative piece of work that was only a partial representation of an entire process?

Instead, I had let the papers sit on my desk and pile up, staring at me accusingly. Students were getting anxious, making comments such as, "Hey, Mr. B., when are we going to get those portfolios back?" and "Last year, Mrs. Jones always gave us our papers back the next day." I knew I needed to grade these things. And now I had to do something fast. My time had run out. But what to do and how to do it? And how could I avoid this last-minute panic next quarter?

A Teacher Responds

Grading something as subjective as writing can be a daunting responsibility. As teachers develop and decide on methods or approaches to address this challenge, it might help first of all to realize that they are not alone in this difficulty. Judges have to decide between consecutive and concurrent sentences. Museum directors have to choose between differently beautiful paintings for an exhibit. Olympic diving judges need to quickly assess the scores on two seemingly equal dives. Football referees must determine whether a facemask penalty is intentional or incidental. And English teachers evaluate the quality of student writing.

Once we accept the idea that some kind of evaluation is needed, how best to proceed? One concept that is a necessary part of any system or method of grading is consistency. As teachers develop an approach to grading, maintaining a consistent application of their philosophy lets the students know what is expected, along with how and why. If the expectations are clearly explained and then adhered to consistently, the writing classroom can be a place of both process-oriented organization and individual, creative freedom.

Since writing instruction involves both process and result, the evaluation of writing should incorporate and reflect both. A system that includes regular conferences with some kind of student accountability during the process of working toward a final or "published" product and then allows the teacher or teacher and student together to make a decision about the success of that final copy can create a fair and understandable method of writing assessment.

After teachers have faced self-doubt or frustration and yet made decisions about writing evaluation, they should trust in their own developing expertise, and they should be able to articulate the decisions they make so that students clearly understand all the components of their classroom writing environment. Using analogies might help the students with this. The teacher might explain, for example, that the writing process could be compared to sports participation. Teams typically have scheduled workouts and practices, and some even encourage individual efforts on an athlete's own time. And every organized team has regular games or matches. The writing classroom can use the same approach: the workouts can be various short writings, designed to practice or highlight specific writing skills or techniques, and they can be read or discussed in teacher-student conferences, with points or scores being given for the efforts and engagement during the process, while the "games" or "matches" can be the final writings, the results of the process and practice. Students learn that both the "workouts" and the "games" are important, even though they have different levels of expectations. Teachers can create grading systems that hold students accountable during all stages of the writing process, allow reward for active participation during the development of a piece of writing, and maintain appropriate expectations for a final product that reflect what students should be able to do, given their abilities and instructional objectives.

Even though it is difficult, teachers should not be afraid to face the grading/assessment challenge. Know who you are, your style and philosophy, and your goals as a teacher of writing. Try to be fair and consistent, clear, and confident. A former principal of mine, who taught instrumental music before becoming an administrator, once asked me, "How can you decide whether an essay deserves a B or a C? It seems so subjective." I responded, "When you taught music, how could you decide who would be second or third chair in the trumpet section?" He indicated that his trained ear, his musical knowledge, and his understanding of the range of abilities possible at the level of high school musicians all assisted him in making that seemingly fuzzy decision. Exactly.

A Teacher Responds

What new teacher hasn't found him- or herself overwhelmed and confused about grading and assessing student work? Early in his career, this teacher saw assessment and instruction as being at odds and viewed grading as a sort of necessary evil imposed on him by people who had little sense of classroom realities. Unfortunately, many share this belief. Becoming clear about the ways that assessment and instruction are inextricably linked can make or break you as an English language arts teacher.

I see grading as part of planning. It's not something to think about at the *end* of an assignment, a unit, or a course, but one of the first things to consider when planning them. You've got to think about the judging before you teach, and then you've got to do the teaching before you judge. What I've learned through trial and error (and trust me, I mean lots of error!) is that the more thought, effort, and planning I can do in advance related to grading and evaluating student work, the better experience the class ends up being for both me and the students. Let's face it; if standards for evaluation are a mystery to us as teachers, they're going to be a mystery to our students. When we are clear about our goals and objectives and share them explicitly, more kids are likely to reach them.

It's a matter of getting the gestalt, of creating (and sharing) the bigger picture *before* we assess. How can we go about doing this? In general, grading considerations are similar whether you're planning individual assignments, entire units, or ways to determine students' overall grades for a class. Questions to ask yourself include the following: What are the overall goals or aims of the course, unit, or assignment? What are the specific learning outcomes for each? Which assignments are really important, will require the most of students, and will be allotted the most class and/or outside time and effort? (Think unit tests, longer writing assignments, more formal projects or presentations, etc.) These are the ones that deserve the most weight when grading and merit the most careful feedback and response from you as a teacher. This work might add up to 65 percent or so of the student's overall grade in the course. Which assignments are minor ones (check tests, short quizzes, daily work, etc.)? Daily work might simply be checked off as done and meeting minimal competency, receiving little or no response from you as the teacher. This work might add up to, say, 15 percent of a student's overall grade in the course. Will you choose to include students in the classroom assessment equation through self-evaluation? How will you factor in attendance, participation, and professionalism? (I value both a lot, so assign 10 percent to each of the two categories.)

Once you've determined your goals and objectives, decided on learning activities, and assigned relative weights and values to each, share them with students on a class syllabus. This will help them see the overall plan for the course and will be useful to them (and to you!)

in remembering which things are most important in the class and therefore merit the most attention, time, and effort.

Those are the bigger, more general considerations and the ones
to decide on first. Next you've got to figure out how to go about grading the major assignments you've identified as integral to your course.
In a classic 1967 article titled "Teaching before We Judge: Planning Assignments in Composition," Richard Larson describes steps I've found
helpful in designing, explaining, and grading specific writing assignments, including the following:

1. Plan the assignment, unit, and course, at least in broad out-
   line form, in advance.

2. Analyze each prospective assignment carefully before you
   give it. Consider what students will need to know in order to
   do well on the assignment.

3. Decide what you must teach now in order to ensure students
   a fair chance to do well on the assignment.

4. Determine what your standards of evaluation on the assignment will be.

5. Draft a written bulletin describing the assignment (or for minor assignments, draft the notes you will use in giving the
   assignment orally).

6. Explain the assignment to students fully, including standards
   for evaluation.

7. (A step I add to Larson's list and find important), provide
   examples and nonexamples of previous students' work on
   the assignment.

8. As part of your explanation of the assignment, allow time for
   students' questions and be ready to point out the pitfalls and
   difficulties they might encounter as they work on the assignment.

9. In evaluating and commenting on papers, make special note
   of where the student has and has not succeeded in reaching
   the explicit objectives of the assignment.

10. Discuss the assignments with students when you return them.
    And finally, don't be afraid to ask students to rewrite.

Steps 4, 6, and 7 of this process tend to be especially challenging
for new teachers. One resource that high school teachers might find
useful in establishing a framework for classroom writing assessment is
NCTE's *Standards Exemplar Series: Assessing Student Performance: Grades
9–12* (Myers & Spalding, 1997). This guide translates the NCTE-IRA
standards into exemplars showing student performance on on-demand

tasks in particular language situations and into portfolios showing student performance on a range of tasks over time. Levels of performance are described through (a) descriptions of on-demand tasks, which represent one or more of the principles in the content standards and which have been tried out in many classrooms; (b) grade-level exemplars of student work on specific tasks requiring particular kinds of knowledge in the English language arts, such as writing reports or responding to literature; (c) rubrics describing the different achievement levels for a given task and situation; and (d) commentaries showing the relationship of each sample to the rubric. Three achievement levels—high, middle, and low—are presented for each on-demand task. This book can be helpful to beginning teachers in determining standards of evaluation on particular assignments and in providing examples and nonexamples of previous students' work on such assignments.

For Further Discussion

1. What is the difference between grading and response? Is this difference significant? How could an awareness of such a difference affect a teacher's writing pedagogy?

2. If you were this teacher's mentor, what advice would you give him to help him at the end of the next grading cycle? How could he set up his class to allow for both effective response and the necessary grades?

3. What are the pros and cons of using a rubric or scoring guide? How can a rubric help students and teachers? Can you think of any situations in which a rubric might be problematic?

Learning Activities

1. In a small group, brainstorm a list of types of writing that should be graded and a corresponding list of writing that you think should not be graded. Then begin to discuss why you have placed the types of writing in the categories that you did.

2. Many teachers create a philosophy of teaching, and in this book you are urged to create your own. Part of such a philosophy often concerns grading issues. Write a short grading philosophy that describes your views of grading in the secondary English classroom, including a definition of grading, why teachers do it, and what connection it has to student learning.

Writing Narrative 4

A staple of good writing instruction is often the use of peer review groups. The purpose of such groups is twofold: (1) to demonstrate to students that writing is a social process and that the responses of readers can be important and useful in determining the effectiveness of a piece of writing, and (2) to help students internalize the evaluation of writing and give them practice in responding to actual texts as well as reflecting on responses provided to them by their peers. But the implementation of peer review groups in the secondary classroom is often much more difficult than it at first appears. Sometimes students use the time in groups to socialize, come to their groups unprepared, or fail to take the activity seriously. The following story narrates the peer review process in one tenth-grade classroom as the teacher attempts to make it instructive for all her student writers. This narrative takes place in a school of about 1,300 students in a suburb of Seattle.

Reviewing Peer Review

While I hear my voice saying, "Okay students, get out your drafts. It's time for peer review," I feel my body preparing for the challenge that will follow. I review in my head: we did lots of prewriting and planning activities, we discussed topic selections, we held workshops, we had drafting time in class and time outside of class, I was available for help, I have a plan for the peer review, and we've gone over it. I've thought of everything, haven't I? Ideally, this *should* work. But experience tells me that all of this doesn't matter because in seconds the reality of the classroom will hit. "You have your peer review sheets. Find a partner and exchange papers. Let's get started." Now.

"Mrs. D., I don't have my draft with me. I left it at home."

"I don't have one either. I never finished what we started in class. Can we go to the commons to write?"

Oh, I'm sure that's what will happen there. Okay, get the ones with no draft started writing. Then make sure everyone has a partner and has started on the peer review.

"Mrs. D., will you do my peer review with me? I don't have a partner."

Doesn't have a partner, or doesn't want one? A lot of these students don't believe a peer can really help them with their writing; after all, what does another fifteen-year-old know about it? And the two girls from Russia are paired up—again. Their language skills aren't the best, and they refuse to work with others who might help them, but they don't know how to help each other, either! Who can I move around to get them some help?

▶

"Mrs. D, who can I work with?"

Katie? What a sweetie. But Katie is a special education student who has no understanding of the concept of a sentence, let alone other aspects of writing. It's hard for a partner to feel she's getting help back from Katie—and it is not easy to help her learn to write. Maybe Sara?

Okay, who else? Barbara doesn't have a partner and is just sitting there. She's told everyone that she's a witch, albeit a good one; it's her religion. Still, she has many of the students nervous—and she doesn't make any overtures either. Who can I get to work with her?

Move around to the groups. Oh, this makes me laugh inside. I love how when I come close to the students the topics change abruptly from the dance or whatever the newest gossip is to some comment about the writing that doesn't make any sense at all. They must think I'm naive as well as deaf and blind. But then, I know many of them have been trained by past experience to see this as a social time. How do I change years of poor experience with peer review? They really believe this is time just for *talking*.

"Mrs. D., I'm done. Will you initial this?"

"Boy, that was fast, Mike. Let me look at it. Your comments on the paper are pretty skimpy. Can you give some elaboration on some of these? And you can't answer the question 'What was the most effective use of imagery and why did it work?' with 'yes.' See if you can give some comments that will help your partner really improve the paper, okay?"

And there's another sign that this is simply an exercise for many of them—the time and thought they put into it. How do I convince them? Keep moving around the room.

Some of these students are really doing a nice job, really helping to improve the writing. Yes! "Good insights, Brad. I think you should take this advice, Terry." I love this part. How can I make it work for the rest of them? And what is Jason doing under the table again? Keep moving.

A Teacher Responds

The stream of consciousness technique this teacher uses to tell her story shows the reader a lot about the difficulties inherent in using peer review in the secondary classroom. She lets us hear her thoughts as she circulates the room on peer review day, and we see students engaging in many behaviors that all of us are probably familiar with: the use of peer review time for socializing, lack of trust in the peer review process, the difficulty of pairing up students in ways that are mutually beneficial, and the tendency for students to rush through the process in order to simply "get done." While peer review has been much touted in professional literature since the 1970s, I often hear teachers at all levels describe the difficulties they have implementing it with any success. I have even heard teachers say they have given up doing peer review because they see at as a waste of time.

So what can these teachers, as well as the teacher in this narrative, do to improve the outcome of peer review? First, I think the teacher might rethink the way she assigns partners for the process. According to the narrative, it appears that the teacher allows the students to pick their own partners, which leads to students choosing friends or to certain students being partnerless time and time again. How about numbering students off or using some other random process to assign partners? Another idea is to ask students to write down (confidentially) on a sheet of paper three peers they would like to work with; then the teacher uses the sheet to assign partners, trying to give students one of their three top choices. This technique allows students some power in choosing, but it also allows the teacher to have a voice in the process and use her knowledge of students' educational needs and how they interact in her class.

I would also suggest thinking about using larger groups, perhaps groups of three or four instead of two. While this increases the time needed for peer review, I think it can alleviate some of the problems the teacher describes. In a group of three or four, for example, a student like Katie might feel less pressure to give complex responses to papers, and the other students in her group might feel that they have received more thorough feedback. Also, a larger group might help with the lack of response, as demonstrated by Mike. If a larger group is used, the teacher could encourage more talk about the papers before the students write comments for the author. Such increased talk might lead Mike and others like him to feel that he has more to say once it comes to writing things down.

Of course, a larger group might actually increase one of this teacher's problems—the use of peer review time for pure socialization. This problem is a tough one. Honestly, I don't think teachers can ever completely stop students from talking about things unrelated to their writing while they are in peer groups, and I don't think they should necessarily want to stop it. Such social talk can increase feelings of community that can lead to more productive group work. I do think the teacher is doing some things to help mitigate this problem, such as circulating among the groups and monitoring their progress as much as possible. One other thing she might try is assigning "roles" to different groups members, much like those used for literature circles (see Chapter 1). One student might be given the role of group leader and her or his job might be to keep the discussion moving along in a productive, relevant way. This student could consult the peer review guide or sheet to help with this task. Other students might assume the roles of note taker, organization specialist, grammarian, thesis detector, etc. In this way, students are held more accountable for their actions in peer review groups.

I'm glad this teacher shared descriptions of students in her class who were engaging in the process successfully. Sometimes it is easy to focus on the negative and forget the good things that are going on in our classes. Perhaps these students could role-play an effective peer review session in front of the whole class in order to demonstrate how it could be done successfully. Such a demonstration can serve the additional purpose of celebrating these students' mastery of the process.

A Teacher Responds

Successful peer reviewing involves a great deal of time preparing students and setting patterns of behavior. I don't think it's enough to give students written guidelines to follow or worksheets to complete during the process. Often the biggest problem is that teachers have simply not spent enough time showing students what to do. The inherent goal of peer review is to encourage students to engage in various discourses about their writing process and developing drafts. I admire Mrs. D.'s persistence and commitment to this ideal but would suggest that she establish acceptable patterns of behavior early by modeling various workshop formats in class, assigning students to ongoing writing groups, writing in-class discovery drafts, and allowing writing groups some choice in adopting their group's workshop format.

Students often don't know exactly what it means to "workshop" a piece of writing and can spend half the class period fidgeting through the process, as this teacher has so perfectly described. Even then, students are often puzzled by exactly what they are expected to do and how this is beneficial for them. If, however, specific workshop formats (such as discovery conferencing, revision workshops, and editing/proofreading workshops) are carefully modeled, then the expectations for behavior and the goals of workshopping are clearer. Mrs. D. could take a piece of her own writing and have students help her revise it on an overhead. As students offer suggestions, she can take the opportunity to clarify the workshop expectations, help students learn how to make positive and productive suggestions, and congratulate students on good ideas and suggestions in order to emphasize how they can help one another.

She might also ask for volunteers to role-play different kinds of writing groups and maybe even bring in some adults to enact different scenarios for students. In either case, participants could dramatize various types of writing groups: one in which the writer reads without offering any elaboration of text or ideas, one in which the writer looks for a central focus by talking through a rough draft, one in which a writer must pose three questions about his or her piece to the rest of the group, one in which the group must reach consensus on three suggestions for the writer, one in which the writer is not allowed to make any comments while another member reads his or her piece aloud, or any other format that the teacher (or students) thinks is appropriate. Or a writing group could be videotaped, and the class could critique the ways in which the group interacted. If we expect our students to conduct effective peer conferences, then we must teach the art of conferencing, just as we teach the craft of writing, and allow students the opportunity to reflect on the purpose of writing workshop.

I would also suggest assigning students to groups of four early in the semester rather than allowing students to partner up, and having the groups meet on a regular basis to establish rapport and continuity. This way the students get to know one another's writing styles and areas of interest and can trace the development of particular pieces. Also, and very important, this strategy establishes some of the expectations and patterns of behavior that have been modeled to make sure they are understood by each group member. Ideally, if the groups meet regularly (once a week? every other Friday? once a month?), they will not have so much "catching up" to excessively chatter about, although I firmly believe that the various discourses inherent in any group activity are essential in creating rapport and community. And with four members, if someone misses class or does not have anything to share, there are still enough participating members to ensure some interaction during the workshopping session.

The groups could be given a choice of workshop format options that the teacher has previously modeled and even a choice of materials on which to focus. I believe it is crucial to allow students to workshop their discovery writing as well as more formal writing assignments. The piece for workshopping doesn't always have to be homework, which invariably some students will not complete. Journal topics, freewriting, questioning, and anything else from class is acceptable material for a workshop, particularly at first when the point is to learn the techniques of the writing conference, not necessarily to work on revising an important piece. If groups practice with pieces and in the group format of their choice, they can develop a higher sense of purpose, authority, and therefore commitment within their groups; when the time comes to workshop a research paper or required writing assignment, students are more prepared to do so.

I think it is worth devoting the necessary class time to emphasize the importance of such activities, including the time that is inevitably spent in conversation. It's a catch-22 of sorts; a teacher should either spend ample time to significantly explore the values and outcomes of peer workshopping or not waste the time spent on less effective methods that actually undermine the process. I once read that developing and adapting any new method into a classroom practice takes at least ten tries. Maybe that's why it's called *practice.* In the end, helping students to develop successful peer workshops is worth the time spent in teaching the procedure and building rapport. I applaud Mrs. D. for persevering, advise her to keep experimenting with options and procedures, and encourage her to involve students in developing the workshop format that best serves their needs.

For Further Discussion

1. In your opinion, what is the role of talk in the secondary classroom? When is it frivolous? When is it important to learning? How do teachers know the difference?

2. What are the goals of peer review? Do you think it should be conducted in the secondary English classroom? Why or why not? If so, are there particular assignments for which it is more applicable?

3. What are some of your memories of collaborative work in high school? When was it effective or enjoyable for you? When was it ineffective? Why?

Learning Activities

1. Create a peer review guide or sheet that you could give to middle school or high school students as they begin the peer review process. What would it say? What kinds of guiding questions or instructions would you give students? Why?

2. In your classroom or in a field experience, experiment with different procedures for grouping students for peer review. For example, (1) allow students to choose groups, (2) choose them

yourself in different ways and (3) vary the size of groups. What differences do you see in the effectiveness of peer review as conducted in each of the groups? Do you think the differences were due, at least in part, to the ways the groups were constructed? How do you know?

In Closing

In this chapter, we have discussed some concepts that are often considered best practices in secondary writing instruction, and we have explored briefly some key controversies. Mostly, however, we have shared stories of teachers as they enacted some of these pedagogical methods and experienced professional dilemmas. Motivating reluctant writers, assigning alternative projects, evaluating effectively, and teaching the writing process through peer review are only a few of the characteristics of effective middle and high school writing teachers. Our point is not that our readers should try to imitate the strategies or approaches suggested by the teacher-responders. On the contrary, we believe that each teacher should develop his or her own understanding of best practice and create a repertoire of strategies that can make those practices come to life in English language arts classrooms.

Our concluding activity asks you to write a philosophy of teaching writing. Write a short (no more than one page) statement describing your philosophy of teaching writing. Begin to answer some of the following questions as you describe your current or future classroom practices in teaching writing and the beliefs that guide them:

1. What kinds of writing do I want students to be able to complete successfully?

2. What is the role of the academic essay in my classes? How will I develop and use authentic audiences and alternative genres?

3. How do I define the writing process? How can I teach my students to develop their writing through process-based activities such as peer review?

4. How much writing will my students do collaboratively? What is the appropriate use of collaboration in my classroom?

5. What is my role as a responder and evaluator of my students' writing? When do I want to focus on editing issues such as spelling, grammar, and mechanics? When should I consider higher-order issues of audience, organization, and content?

Additional Texts about the Teaching of Writing

Books

Anson, Chris M., Joan Graham, David A. Jolliffe, Nancy S. Shapiro, and Carolyn H. Smith. (1993). *Scenarios for Teaching Writing: Contexts for Discussion and Reflective Practice.* Urbana, IL: National Council of Teachers of English.

> This is a book of cases or stories depicting different events, issues, or problems that university writing instructors commonly face, along with questions for discussion.

Black, Laurel, Donald A. Daiker, Jeffery Sommers, and Gail Styhall (Eds.). (1994). *New Directions in Portfolio Assessment: Reflective Practice, Critical Theory, and Large-Scale Scoring.* Portsmouth, NH: Boynton/Cook.

> This collection of essays describes and discusses portfolio assessment in secondary schools and its pedagogical and political implications.

Bleich, David. (1998). *Know and Tell: A Writing Pedagogy of Disclosure, Genre, and Membership.* Portsmouth, NH: Boynton/Cook.

> Bleich takes a postprocess approach to writing pedagogy and explores how writing classrooms and student language use are affected by the material realities of students' lives, including socioeconomic, cultural, racial, ethnic, and gender identities. Bleich also explores the grading of student writing through a postmodern lens and how classroom "discomfort" can sometimes be the catalyst for learning.

Elbow, Peter. (1973). *Writing without Teachers.* New York: Oxford University Press.

> A landmark book outlining a student-centered writing pedagogy, Elbow's text focuses on peer response groups and prewriting/invention strategies. This is a wonderful introduction to process writing and how to teach students to provide substantive feedback in writing groups.

Fulkerson, Richard. (1996). *Teaching the Argument in Writing.* Urbana, IL: National Council of Teachers of English.

> This book translates classical rhetoric and Toulmin's model of argument into clear, accessible language and suggests ways they

can be incorporated in the high school writing class. It includes discussions of claims, fallacies, and logic.

Harris, Muriel. (1986). *Teaching One-to-One: The Writing Conference.* Urbana, IL: National Council of Teachers of English.

Harris provides theory and rationale for conference teaching as well as specific suggestions for conducting effective writing conferences with students. This text is a practical application of composition pedagogy to the teacher-student conference or tutorial.

Hillocks, George Jr. (1995). *Teaching Writing as Reflective Practice.* New York: Teachers College Press.

Hillocks takes an innovative look at the writing process and defines both writing and teaching as processes of inquiry that can be improved on through reflective thinking. He suggests teachers use "frame experiments" to craft classroom activities, try them out, and then assess their effectiveness in helping students learn to write.

Lane, Barry. (1993). *After the End: Teaching and Learning Creative Revision.* Portsmouth, NH: Heinemann.

This readable and entertaining book provides numerous practical revision strategies for secondary students, including "exploding a moment" and "shrinking a century." Lane's ideas are crafted more with the middle school student in mind, but his creative approach and emphasis on narrative writing has much secondary classroom potential.

Lanham, Richard A. (1992). *Revising Prose* (3rd ed.). New York: Macmillan.

Lanham offers practical suggestions for tightening and revising prose, including his "paramedic method" and other sentence-based strategies. Although he focuses on sentence-level issues, his emphasis is on improving style, not just on issues of editing or correctness.

Lindemann, Erika. (1995). *A Rhetoric for Writing Teachers* (3rd ed.). New York: Oxford University Press.

Lindemann outlines what secondary English teachers should know about rhetorical history and theory and why knowing it will improve their practice. In addition to giving a brief history of classical rhetoric, she applies many of the ideas to the contemporary English class.

North, Stephen M. (1987). *The Making of Knowledge in Composition: Portrait of an Emerging Field.* Upper Montclair, NJ: Boynton/Cook.

This book is often cited as a groundbreaking text in composition studies. It is a discussion of various forms of research and inquiry that are conducted in the discipline and how each of them has enriched understandings of the teaching of writing. One of North's goals is to establish composition studies as a discipline by outlining the most significant research and related theoretical positions of those who teach and study writing. He also succeeds in giving a nice overview of the types of research (for example, qualitative, experimental, and textual) compositionists conduct in their field.

Shaughnessy, Mina P. (1977). *Errors and Expectations: A Guide for the Teacher of Basic Writing.* New York: Oxford University Press.

This landmark text examines how common errors in student writing can be linked to an underlying logic that can be identified, and modified, through error analysis and focused instruction. Shaughnessy's goal is to see basic writers not as less intelligent than their "regular" counterparts but as simply working from their own set of language rules that do not correlate with those of Standard Edited English.

Soven, Margot. (1998). *Teaching Writing in Middle and Secondary Schools: Theory, Research, and Practice.* Boston: Allyn and Bacon.

Soven's textbook includes chapters on teaching the writing process, creating assignments, responding to student texts, and evaluating student work in the middle and secondary school. Overall, the text is an effective and readable introduction to the discipline of English education and the practice of English teaching.

Tchudi, Stephen (Ed.). (1997). *Alternatives to Grading Student Writing.* Urbana, IL: National Council of Teachers of English.

Contributors to Tchudi's book explore ways to respond to and evaluate various kinds of student texts in nontraditional ways. Some ideas include parent response, peer response, outcomes-based assessment, and portfolio assessment.

Tchudi, Susan J., and Stephen N. Tchudi. (1999). *The English Language Arts Handbook: Classroom Strategies for Teachers.* Portsmouth, NH: Boynton/Cook.

This text, similar in structure to Soven's, includes pedagogical and theoretical guidance for secondary school teachers of literature and writing, including discussions of instructional planning, reader response to literature, teaching grammar, and the writing process.

Thompson, Thomas C. (Ed.). (2002). *Teaching Writing in High School and College: Conversations and Collaborations.* Urbana, IL: National Council of Teachers of English.

This book is a collection of essays describing and providing models for university-secondary school collaboration concerning the teaching of writing. Issues addressed include preservice teacher education, definitions of effective writing at secondary and postsecondary levels, and ways secondary and university faculty can work together to better prepare student writers for professional life.

Zinsser, William. (1998). *On Writing Well: The Classic Guide to Writing Nonfiction* (6th ed.). New York: HarperCollins.

This famous text about writing effectively is noteworthy for its attention to clarity and style as well as to the complexities of the writing process. A must-read for student and adult writers, Zinsser speaks as a skilled writer giving advice to would-be authors.

Electronic Resources

The National Writing Project
www.writingproject.org/

The National Writing Project started with a single institute for inservice teachers in Berkeley, California, in 1972 and has grown to include 175 sites in all fifty states, Washington D.C., Puerto Rico, and the U.S. Virgin Islands. The project began as a grassroots effort to encourage "teachers to teach teachers" about the composing process and writing to learn. The Web site includes access to NWP publications, presentations, workshops, institutes, and support networks.

Purdue University Online Writing Lab (OWL)
http://owl.english.purdue.edu/

This Web site includes online tutorials for student writers and provides access to instructional materials for teacher use.

Writing Across the Curriculum
www.engl.niu.edu/wac/

> This Web site includes a brief history of the Writing Across the Curriculum (WAC) movement and provides links to related sites. Teachers interested in WAC should also consult the books of Toby Fulwiler (1987, 1990 [with A. Young]).

The Writing Instructor
http://writinginstructor.com

> The *Writing Instructor* is an online journal about the teaching of writing at all developmental and grade levels. It includes interactive chats, video, images, Web links, and traditional written texts about writing instruction.

3 Narratives about Teaching Language and Grammar

Perhaps no topic creates as much controversy within our field as that of how to teach language and grammar. Harry Noden in *Image Grammar: Using Grammatical Structures to Teach Writing* (1999) describes discussions of grammar in the teacher's lounge "as a little like stepping between two 350-pound NFL linemen just after the ball is snapped" (p. vii). From our experiences in our classrooms and schools, we can vouch for the ferocity of the debates, in both local and national settings. Often these debates are oversimplified because educators are divided into two camps. In one corner are the traditionalists, who value grammar unconditionally and teach it as a separate and distinct part of their curricula. In the other corner are the teachers who know and accept the research demonstrating that formal, isolated grammar instruction does not correlate with students' ability to communicate, think, or develop ideas that successfully reach specific audiences. They may, however, have taken this knowledge to the extreme and decided to eliminate grammar from their curricula altogether. For us, grammar must be connected to language use and communicative goals. To separate the two is to decontextualize grammar from communication and make it irrelevant to our students. But we also believe that there is a definitive place for grammar and language instruction in secondary English classrooms, as long as the chosen instructional method is supported by sound, evidence-based pedagogical theory.

Stephen Tchudi and Susan Tchudi (1999) break down current views on grammar by classifying the current roles of teachers as those of *enforcer* (the teacher who accepts only Standard English in his or her classroom and works as a caretaker of the English language), *bidialectalist* (someone who recognizes and respects the dialect of students while trying to "nudge" them toward Standard English), or *expansionist* (the teacher who avoids the enforcement of a standard dialect and seeks to evaluate language as it is used in various rhetorical contexts) (pp. 212–13).

While we understand this debate, we believe that these categories do not have to be mutually exclusive. All of these views argue valid points and reflect theoretical perspectives that can lead to exemplary practice in the teaching of grammar and language. Instead, we believe that the most important element of teaching grammar and language is developing a personal/professional theory regarding your beliefs about the issue. If you do not want to bring grammar into your classroom explicitly or overtly, then you should follow through with your decision because you have a theory and philosophy that guides what you do. Likewise, if you see a place for grammatical discussions and exercises, you should be able to justify your practices in terms of current theory and research about language acquisition and best practices in the teaching of English language arts.

We believe that best practice probably lies somewhere between the opposing theoretical positions, and the way we have chosen to title this chapter reflects this belief: notice that we call the chapter "narratives about teaching language *and* grammar" instead of simply "narratives about teaching grammar." Grammar and language use are inseparable and therefore should not be taught as separate entities. Grammar (i.e., parts of speech, labeling and recognizing types of phrases and clauses, and usage rules such as subject-verb agreement, verb tense, and split infinitives) and related syntactic skills are only relevant in a communicative context that reflects and affects a set of material, real-world characteristics (e.g., interactions in the workplace and between friends or family members). Language skills and communicative sophistication are far more complex than traditional grammar instruction often makes them seem; in fact, language use is closely connected to individual and social identity development as well as to an individual's success in living and working in the dominant culture.

Since the early twentieth century, educational research has shown that isolated, formal, and terminology-laden grammar instruction is not linked to improved student writing. Constance Weaver (1996), for example, summarizes these findings throughout her book *Teaching Grammar in Context*. To paraphrase Weaver,

1. Studying grammar as a set of terms is not the best use of instructional time if you want students' writing to improve.

2. Young children acquire the major grammatical constructions of their language naturally and intuitively, without direct instruction. Therefore, they do not need to be taught formal grammar in order to write or to read.

3. Wide reading may be one of the best ways to learn grammar; even listening to literature read aloud can facilitate the acquisition of syntax and vocabulary. Writing, of course, is also important. But students will not necessarily learn new grammatical constructions from writing unless teachers demonstrate the relevance of knowledge of grammatical concepts and skills to "real" language use.

4. Analyzing language and learning to label its parts—the focus of traditional grammar instruction—is much less helpful to writers than engaging in the process of writing or completing sentence-generating, -combining, or -manipulating exercises (p. 179).

Perhaps the best-known statement condemning the teaching of grammar outside of the context of student writing comes from Braddock, Lloyd-Jones, and Schoer (1963) in their much-cited meta-analysis of research on the teaching of writing:

> In view of the widespread agreement of research studies based upon many types of students and teachers, the conclusions can be stated in strong and unqualified terms: the teaching of formal grammar has a negligible or, because it usually displaces some instruction and practice in actual composition, even a harmful effect on the improvement of writing. (pp. 37–38)

Despite the preponderance of evidence showing that teaching traditional, isolated, or formal grammar has no perceived effect on writing ability, many teachers continue to teach it as it has been taught for generations—through handbook drills, memorization, and diagramming or labeling exercises. So why do some teachers ignore the evidence against the teaching of formal grammar? There could be several reasons, including the continued inclusion of grammatical terminology on some standardized tests, the feeling that grammar is a tradition in the teaching of English and therefore there must be some value in it, and the ease with which grammar exercises can be assigned and graded. Whatever the reasons for the continued teaching of formal or decontextualized grammar, we hope that the narratives in this chapter encourage you to reflect on your beliefs and make theoretically sound curricular decisions concerning the teaching of grammar and language in your present or future classes.

What Is *Good* Language and Grammar Instruction?

Zemelman, Daniels, and Hyde (1998) clearly make the point that grammar is best taught in the context of actual writing, and Constance Weaver (1996, 1998) asserts that grammar is contextual and must be taught in ways that are constructive or as part of a "building up" of language sophistication or of a communicative text rather than in ways that are analytical or part of a "breaking down" of sentences into their parts for isolated analysis. What this means in the classroom, however, can vary from teacher to teacher depending on his or her theoretical orientation regarding grammar. In keeping with a more conservative perspective, a teacher might teach minilessons about parts of speech during the writing process. Oftentimes minilessons might be conducted as part of a daily exercise that examines a sentence or two that have no connection to anything else students are doing in class. In a more innovative or contemporary approach, students might create their own grammars for specific audiences or purposes or grammars that are consistent with their home dialects. A variety of practices in between these two extremes can exemplify the contextual nature of grammar and its use as a productive tool for communication. Minilessons can be taught, for example, in response to identified student problems and therefore grow out of the context of student writing. Consider the following list of best practices in language and grammar instruction as you reflect on your developing teaching philosophy. As usual, if you want to read more about any of these approaches or theories, please see the annotated bibliography at the end of this chapter.

Characteristics of Effective Secondary Language and Grammar Pedagogy

Recently we eavesdropped as a group of practicing and preservice teachers discussed teaching grammar. The following points emerged, each with its own philosophical and practical relevance. We borrowed from this conversation to establish our list of characteristics of effective language and grammar pedagogy.

1. Discussions of Grammar Should Empower Students to Explore Their Language and Become Better Communicators. Grammar and language should be seen as tools for facilitating communication in various situations rather than as sets of rules to be learned and reproduced on a test. Harry Noden's *Image Grammar* (1999) provides an excellent example of how such an approach can be enacted in the classroom. Noden understands grammar metaphorically as he compares writing with painting and an artist's brushstrokes with grammatical elements, namely the participle, the absolute, the appositive, adjectives, and action verbs. By thinking of grammar as similar to an artist's tools, a writer can begin to see its mastery as a way to create effective, powerful texts, not just as a necessary evil for those wanting to do well on standardized tests. When language and grammar study empowers rather than disconnects, students will not believe that their home dialects are inferior to the privileged, standard one; instead, they will understand that while they may have to use Standard English for certain rhetorical tasks, they can also communicate effectively and powerfully in their home dialects.

2. Language Must Be Taught in a Context. Too many teachers approach grammar as a set of indisputable, immutable, unchangeable rules that provide a set of terms to be memorized. The reality of language is that it changes and evolves over time and meets the needs of a rhetorical situation (for an example, look at your local McDonald's drive-"thru" or try to order a "soda" in the upper Midwest). There are several strategies that teachers can use in the classroom to teach grammar and usage without focusing on isolated terminology. Teachers can, for example, ask students to listen to the reading of a passage with interesting or unusual punctuation and grammar and write down what they hear, inserting punctuation and beginning and ending sentences where they think it is necessary. Then students can share their responses and compare notes. The point is not to see who wrote the passage the closest to the original; the point is to discuss the various ways it was written and the changes in meaning that resulted from the variations. A teacher might ask, "Why did you use a semicolon here and not a period?"; "What is the difference between using a dash and a comma?"; "How does a colon change the tone of this sentence?" As a result of this kind of exploration, such editorial decisions take on rhetorical significance.

3. Language Lessons Should Encourage Students to Explore the Language around Them and Learn about Its Complexities. Language is an important part of everyday life and is essential to human interactions and identities; therefore, it should be treated with wonder and sincere interest. Discussions of grammar and language should encourage students to recognize interesting aspects of language use throughout their lives—in dialect, on street signs, on the radio—and learn to appreciate the importance of language use beyond the classroom. The message here is to nurture in our students the desire to notice the language around them and understand it not as part of an isolated school activity but as an important part of their daily lives.

4. Language or Grammar Lessons Should Be Integrated with Other Instruction. It doesn't take a leap forward in knowledge to realize that separate and isolated grammar instruction typically does not engage most students, in particular because it doesn't directly connect to communication. The quarterlong grammar "unit" is rarely a success. A better practice is to integrate grammar and language instruction into regular classroom processes and procedures. While it may not be teaching language "in the context" of student writing, some teachers have had great success with activities such as McDougal, Littell's Daily Oral Language series in which students edit or correct short prose passages together as a class, usually at the beginning of a period. Such an activity becomes part of daily classroom routine yet does not consume the entire period for days at a time. Daily Oral Language is also useful because the sentences are corrected so that they make more sense or become clearer to the reader. Additionally, students can examine grammatical constructions in the literature they read and analyze how the sentence-level choices the author makes affect meaning. Then students might imitate these stylistic or syntactic choices when writing their own stories or essays. We recommend such practices as well as other activities that connect grammar to actual reading, writing, and speaking.

5. Language and Grammar Should Not Be Ignored but Understood as Lower-Order Concerns in Writing and Communication. In the context of teaching writing, this may be the most important point about grammar instruction. There is an old adage that "you don't change the tires on a car that is missing an engine." The same holds true for the relationship between grammar, language, and writing. Teachers should not focus their responses and instruction on the lower-order concerns of grammatical appropriateness and language, style, and fluency if there is work to be done on higher-order issues of audience, purpose, and genre, among others. Grammar and language issues are generally a lower-order concern, one of importance but also one that does not take precedence in the language arts classroom over the rhetorical goals of a writer or that writer's process of inquiry as he or she develops ideas in a piece of writing. Grammatical concepts and language instruction should not prevent students from communicating or from developing fluency. Instead, they should help students become more confident and more fluent in their discourse.

Controversies in Language and Grammar Instruction

We also heard from teachers about some approaches to teaching language or grammar that they have attempted in their classrooms (or have seen done by colleagues) and do not recommend to others. These "don'ts" are often supported by educational research, and they highlight some of the major controversies in our profession about the teaching of language and grammar. So again we will borrow from our overheard conversation to list and explain some of the major disciplinary controversies about which we think you should be aware.

1. Teaching an Isolated Grammar Lesson (a Unit Devoted to Analytic Grammar) versus Teaching Grammar as Contextual. As we have previously stated, some teachers believe that teaching grammar outside the context of teaching writing has value in and of itself: as a set of skills or terms to be defined, as a body of knowledge that all "literate" students should know, or as a means of teaching analytical thinking. We can see situations in which this might be true—for example, in a structural linguistics course. In high school or middle school English classrooms, however, most educators we know would say that they teach grammar and language skills in order to improve writing; and, as we have already stressed, research and theory see little connection between the teaching of traditional, isolated grammar and improved writing practice. To complicate the issue even further, teaching and evaluating grammar exercises can seem easy to teachers; it is relatively simple to assign handbook exercises and then quickly grade them, since answers are clearly right or wrong. Because secondary teachers are consistently overworked and have too many students in their classes, teaching grammar out of context can be a tempting way to keep students busy and minimize the grading load. We believe that a restructuring of schools to reduce class sizes and increase the planning and preparation time for teachers could best solve this problem, but this solution might be idealistic for the time being and is certainly outside the scope of most individual teachers. Interestingly enough, in a recent issue of the *English Journal,* teacher Lynn Sams (2003) argues that even sentence diagramming can be taught contextually and rhetorically. So perhaps even teachers who, for whatever reason, continue to use more traditional instructional methods can approach grammar instruction contextually and therefore ensure its relevance for students.

2. Devoting an Entire Unit to Grammar Study versus Integrating It into the Curriculum. This debate is similar to that discussed in the previous point, but it is really a curricular issue rather than an individual lesson plan issue. Separating the curriculum into discrete "units"—the poetry unit, the writing unit, the grammar unit, etc.—has been a common way of organizing classes for many generations and is reinforced by the arrangements of many textbooks and curriculum guides. This kind of discrete unit approach, however, is not completely consistent with an interdisciplinary or integrated approach to curriculum. In an integrated approach, curricula are organized thematically, and these themes are selected because they reflect issues of interest and concern to adolescents. In an interdisciplinary approach to curriculum, the disciplines are integrated in instructional units; when teaching a young adult novel such as Linda Sue Park's *A Single Shard,* for example, the historical context of its setting, twelfth-century Korea, could be explored, and the students might conduct research about (and even create) Korean celadon pottery since the novel's main character strives to be a potter. While integrated and interdisciplinary approaches are most common in middle schools, sometimes they are also enacted in high schools, where many educators believe they result in increased learning because students see more relevance in the material presented and they are able to engage in many types of activities that tap multiple intelligences. In such approaches, grammar and language instruction could be related to the theme of the unit, and once related to such a larger issue or idea, grammatical and linguistic concepts might be more interesting to students. In the *A Single Shard* example, students might compare the sentence structure Park uses to represent the speech of the old and the young characters in the novel. They might consider why the older characters seem to use different vocabulary and even different types of sentences (e.g., simple, complex) from those of the teenagers.

3. English Teachers as Grammar Experts versus English Teachers as Experts in Communication. The teachers we overheard discussing grammar stated that it was problematic to set yourself up as a grammarian—the person everyone approaches with grammar questions or the teacher with whom students are afraid to communicate because they are scared of being judged as lacking grammatical knowledge. If you aren't careful, you might become the "walking handbook" of grammar and language rules that colleagues and students come to for "answers" to grammatical questions. The fact is that no one is perfect, and no one can memorize every grammar "rule" so that it can be accessed at will—not even an English teacher. Eventually you will give an incorrect answer or no answer at all. This is not a problem if you have not defined your role as that of the grammar expert; perhaps you are simply a source of knowledge who can either provide suggestions or direct people to resources where answers can be found. In this way, students will begin to understand that grammar and language skills are learned over time and that their level of "correctness" is variable and dependent on a rhetorical context.

4. Focusing on Grammar as Being "Right" or "Wrong" versus Understanding the Social and Political Dimensions of Grammar. In 1974 the Conference on College Composition and Communication (CCCC) adopted a position statement called "Students' Right to Their Own Language." This position statement argues that students at all levels have the right to communicate in their native dialects and describes the unfair ideological hierarchies often created by and reflected in the educational and social prominence of Standard English. The CCCC committee suggested that teachers respect the home dialects of students and teach them how to "dialect shift," whereby they select either their home or standard dialect when completing different writing tasks addressing different audiences. Many modern composition theorists have embraced the idea of respect for dialectical diversity and extend the CCCC position statement by arguing that teachers should not only teach options but also interrogate *why* options exist and the ideological and cultural significance of choosing among them. Consequently, the English teacher in the writing classroom becomes more than the purveyor of information about dialectical and grammatical choices; he becomes a critical educator who teaches students, who often use nonstandard dialects, about the ideological and political context of language use. Instead, for example, of simply explaining to students that at least two types of language may exist (i.e., their home language and the usually privileged and "correct" academic language), the teacher asks student writers to analyze their audience and actively select the dialect in which to complete an assignment. Finally, a teacher may ask students to reflect on the reasons for their choice and the rhetorical effect they anticipate it will have.

5. Making Grammar a Central Part of Writing Evaluations (e.g., 5 errors = D; 10 errors = F) versus Understanding It as a Lower-Order Concern. As we discussed at length earlier in this chapter and in Chapter 2, grammatical errors (as well as punctuation, spelling, and usage issues), while a vital concern in ensuring the effectiveness of a final draft, are not the most important aspects of the writing process or the most important elements of a successful piece of writing. When you're creating rubrics or scoring guides, we recommend that grammar, usage, punctuation, and spelling appear toward the end of the guide so as to connote their lower-order nature and to suggest that fewer points be attached to their correct use than to the development of ideas or the effectiveness of an argument.

In conclusion, we do not believe that there is one right way to approach grammar in the English classroom. Instead, there are many ways to integrate the teaching of grammar and language into English language arts curricula in theoretically sound and effective ways. In this chapter, we give an overview of what theory and research teaches about grammar instruction in the secondary school in the hopes that this over-view helps you develop a philosophy about teaching grammar and lan-guage that is not hamstrung by an extreme ideology.

Narratives

Here we present four narratives about the teaching of grammar and language in the secondary school. These stories address different prob-lems associated with teaching grammar and language, including stu-dent apathy, teacher boredom, and how to integrate a whole language philosophy of teaching with grammar instruction. In the first story, "Tale of the Reformed Grammarian," a teacher expresses his frustration with traditional grammar instruction and his feeling that such instruction is not improving his students' writing. The second narrative, "Here's Your Grammar Unit," is written from the perspective of a first-year teacher who is provided with an intact "grammar unit" and is expected to teach it to her ninth graders. The third story, "The New Approach," tells of an English as a second language (ESL) teacher's experiences teaching grammar concepts while trying to be consistent with a whole language approach to instruction, and the last narrative, "Why Do I Bother? Teach-ing Minilessons to Student Writers," asks the question, "How do I help students recognize and correct their own grammar errors?"

Language and Grammar Narrative 1

Often we hear stories from teachers who have been teaching for sev-eral years using a traditional method of grammar instruction and not getting the results they expect. This often leads to a reevaluation of what works with language in the classroom. In this story, we see a veteran teacher beginning to rethink his beliefs about approaching grammar and language and deciding to stop teaching grammar altogether. But is he going too far? Or not far enough? This story takes place in a suburban school in central Michigan.

Tale of the Reformed Grammarian

I feel as though I should begin this as a confessional: "Hi, I'm Dave and I used to be a grammarian." The crowd could respond, "Hi, Dave. We respect you." Or even more appropriately, they could help me with my twelve-step program, freeing me from grammatical correctness by replying with "ain't" or "We wouldn't of judged you any-how." Thank goodness that's past. Here's my tale:

One dark December morning I was at the end of my rope. I was reading my latest set of essays, red pencil in hand, and gritting my teeth. Error after error after error. And *after* we had peer edited, cre-ated "grammar notebooks," and worked on grammar almost daily for three months. Three long months of my teaching life. Gone down the tubes. My class just didn't get it. So I gave up.

Yup. I waved the white flag. I gave in to the demons of the "antigrammar" brigade I had been resisting all these years. In retro-spect, a better metaphor would be "changing tack" since I didn't give up as much as I changed direction, but it didn't seem so at the time.

I stopped teaching grammar. Cold turkey. No explanation, no discussion. No more grammar handbooks, daily editing, or discus-sions of the virtues of the different types of verbs. No more adjectives, adverbs, phrases, and clauses, and I buried my well-worn *Schoolhouse Rock* grammar video under some old journals.

But now what was I going to do? I taught literature and writ-ing and went on with my daily teaching life as if grammar didn't exist. And you know what happened? Nothing. Nothing bad, that is. My kids seemed to enjoy writing more, and we spent time that I used to dedicate to grammar talking about interesting things in the literature we were reading and doing more projects that had us creatively rep-resenting our findings. I also was able to do more writing with my students. We wrote journals, published a class newsletter on litera-ture we had read, put on short plays based on scenes we had read (or created scenarios that "could have" happened), and generally had a good time.

Grammar is now banned from my classroom. We're too busy with other things. But I still have that nagging feeling—shouldn't I be doing more?

A Teacher Responds

I really respect this writer's ability to question his long-standing com-mitment to teaching formal grammar. It sounds as though he spent way too much time in the grammarian mode, critiquing student papers for correctness. I've often felt that we sometimes focus on grammar in or-der to feel as though we have "content" to pass on to our students and brag about to our colleagues in the teacher's lounge. I'm glad that he sees the problems inherent in this approach.

I also applaud his decision to use the opportunity presented by removing grammar to expand his teaching practices to include interesting ways to approach literature and writing. I'm excited when I see teachers who are already established in their practices break free and enliven their classrooms.

My other response, however, is that he may have gone too far in his surrender to the no-grammar approach. I remember that when I first learned about using computers in my classroom, I was convinced I was never going to have students write with pen and paper again. I was like a fresh convert to a new religion. I was determined to shed my classroom of those "old" practices and start anew. I would ask this teacher to take time to look at some of the practices he used previously and try to combine them with his newfound enthusiasm for the no-grammar approach. In other words, perhaps he could still teach some minilessons about grammatical issues with which his students seem to be having problems when they write. Perhaps he could integrate a five-minute Daily Oral Language series exercise into the beginning of most class periods. I'm always guided by the concept of using language and grammar to help students become better writers and communicators. This doesn't mean that I drill grammar into their brains or assign countless handbook exercises. It does mean, however, that I use grammar as a means of improving their writing and teach it in the context of specific writing assignments. In my classroom, there is always a place for peer revision, editing, and discussions of grammar, even if we do talk in terms of "What is appropriate for your audience?" or "Which syntactic choice is the most effective stylistically?" rather than "What is correct?"

A Teacher Responds

I think it's great that this teacher has come to the decision he has. I wish some people in my school would make the same conversion. We can, however, do so much with grammar without teaching grammar in the traditional or formal sense. In my high school class, we approach grammar and style by reading published texts similar in genre to ones students are writing and then discussing syntactic style and grammatical choices that are best suited for the rhetorical situation. We might examine, for example, an editorial in our local newspaper, discuss the form and style of this genre (for example, short paragraphs, sentences with catchy beginnings, opinions clearly stated early in the piece, etc.), and then compare it to a similar text published in a newsmagazine or appearing on a local television news program. In this way, my students can explore and describe stylistic nuances that exist even within examples of the same genre depending on their purpose and intended audience. Additionally, students can examine grammatical structures in a work of literature and how the syntax the author chooses affects the meaning, tone, or mood of the piece. Consequently, examinations of grammar are intimately connected to meaning. We also look at grammar gaffes in published writing and talk about how these errors can hurt the credibility or "ethos" of the author. Thus, we come to the understanding that grammar *does* matter but not as much as understanding its communicative context and how this context affects the grammatical and stylistic choices authors make.

I would recommend that this teacher explore his instinct that he could do more. He's headed in the right direction, but now it's time to qualify his new approach with more pedagogical substance than simply insisting on "no grammar." While grammatical correctness might be considered less important than developing other writing skills, teaching students to use Standard English correctly is still a worthy goal of English teachers and one we must pursue if, for no other reason, we are to meet the demands of high-stakes standardized tests. But I think we can strike a balance between believing that we should teach grammar and language skills and teaching formal, traditional, and isolated grammatical terminology. One way of striking such a balance could be to ask students to engage in stylistic analyses as described earlier; another approach might involve sentence combining or manipulating activities for which students are given short "kernel" sentences and asked to put them together in various ways. While completing these activities, students experiment with using coordinating and subordinating clauses and modifiers and hence often increase their syntactic sophistication (see Hunt [1966, 1970, 1977] for more details about research supporting the benefits of sentence-combining activities). In short, while I applaud this teacher's renunciation of formal grammar instruction, I urge him to continue thinking about theoretically sound and effective ways to teach grammar and language skills.

For Further Discussion

1. In this case, we see a teacher move from one extreme philosophical position to another. What could he do that would help him develop a more centered theory of grammar instruction? How could he approach grammar in a way that does not ignore it completely but instead focuses on the writing and communication of his students?

2. The teacher in the narrative is concerned with "other things" such as interesting writing activities and innovative group

projects. What are some ways that grammar instruction could be appropriately integrated into these sorts of projects?

3. What do you think about the 1974 CCCC position statement called "Students' Right to Their Own Language"? Do you agree with the opinions it expresses? How do you see such a philosophical position affecting grammar and language instruction in the secondary school?

Learning Activities

1. Write about how you would define yourself as a teacher of grammar and language. Are you an enforcer, or more traditional grammar instructor? Or do you believe in bidialectalism or expansionist concepts? At this point in your career, how will you address issues of grammar and language use in your classroom?

2. With a partner, develop one or more lesson plans that integrate the teaching of grammar and language into other instructional units, such as a unit about a literary text. You might, for example, envision teaching a text that uses dialectical variety among characters as a way to make a point about social or economic inequities (i.e., Mark Twain's *The Adventures of Huckleberry Finn* or Maya Angelou's *I Know Why the Caged Bird Sings*).

Language and Grammar Narrative 2

In this story, we see a typical scenario as a new teacher describes her experiences translating her beliefs about teaching grammar in context in a situation in which she is expected to teach grammar in traditional ways. Establishing a professional identity as a first-year teacher is difficult, and the mentor system can be helpful in this process. This teacher, however, is given some rather directive, and theoretically unsound, pedagogical advice by a mentor. What is she to do? This story takes place in a large, suburban, midwestern high school.

Here's Your Grammar Unit

I guess I should have seen it coming. Although like a bad relationship, I think I was hoping it would just fade away. At my school, each first-year teacher has a "mentor teacher," an experienced colleague to guide the new teacher through the first year. I met my mentor teacher, Susan, in June, shortly after I was offered the job. She was smart, enthusiastic, and funny. I was sure we were going to become good friends. I felt lucky to be at a school where they don't just give you the keys and hope you succeed.

▶

Here's the deal, though. At the end of our first conversation, she pulled out her binder of grammatical exercises and said, "Here's your grammar unit. All the ninth-grade teachers do it. Give me a call if you need any help with it." Being polite and nice (and intimidated), I just smiled and accepted the "gift."

"Maybe it's not so bad," I thought to myself as I pulled the spiral-bound behemoth towards me. Oh, yes it was . . . pages upon pages of nouns, verbs, phrases, clauses, and other things I had never been taught in college and remembered hating in high school. I spent years discussing Shakespeare, not diagramming sentences. I knew there was something wrong with this "unit" idea, but I wasn't sure what else to do.

It turns out the entire ninth-grade English department starts off the year with a three-week grammar unit. We all do similar activities at the same time, although I was told that I could be as "creative" as I wanted—as long as I finished in exactly three weeks. Ha!

I did it. It worked, kind of. I think I benefited from an extended "honeymoon" period with my kids because I was young. I tried a few minor changes. We kept our exercises in notebooks that I had everyone turn into handbooks. I'm planning to use them as individual resource books when they do writing projects later. And if a grammar question comes up, instead of giving the answer, I can tell a student to refer to his or her handbook. I also had them decorate the covers and personalize them a bit. This helped occupy students who were ahead of the rest of the class.

As I look back on it, though, I'm really disappointed in myself. I didn't get into the profession to teach things I found repulsive and boring as a student. I wanted to share my love of language and literature with my students. And it took me some time to develop a classroom community after this stutter-step beginning.

I'm already planning for next year. I'll still do a grammar project—kind of. There's no need to rock the boat too much. I'm thinking of having my students write personal essays, something like "my most embarrassing moment" or memoirs of important events in our lives. I'm hoping this can be a fun writing assignment that we can link to some easy-to-read short stories and poems. Then we can write and share our writing during a class read-around or on a bulletin board. The grammar? No problem. We'll do minilessons at the beginning of each class and focus them on "big problems" that are evi-

▶

dent in the students' writing projects. Then we'll add these issues to our grammar handbooks.

Will it work? I hope so, because I'm not doing the grammar unit again.

A Teacher Responds

This is an excellent example of someone beginning to come into her own as a teacher and develop a singular sense of what "good" teaching is. I think she's definitely on the right track with her interpretation of the opening unit. I'm concerned that her fellow teachers accept the grammar unit as a normal part of their curriculum. My response is not so much about this writer's teaching as it is about a professional role she needs to play in her school and her professional interactions with colleagues.

I think she is clearly coming to understand the idea of teaching grammar in context and is right to integrate it with writing. I would encourage her to continue to experiment with her beginning-of-the-year activities. Over time I would hope that she sees that grammar instruction is not as important as community building with a new class. If she wants to include grammar at the beginning of the year, I would suggest making it a more interesting project, one in which students learn to examine their home dialects or the syntax or linguistic style evident in various settings and contexts, including perhaps text on road signs, on fast-food menus, in e-mail or chat room exchanges, etc. Then they could springboard this into a discussion of questions such as What is grammar? What is Standard English? Where do grammar rules come from? Why were they created?

As I said earlier, though, I'm actually more concerned about her relationship with her colleagues. There are certain times in a teacher's career when a situation demands that she step forward to share with colleagues what she is doing. I think this could be a situation in which such sharing could be appropriate. Perhaps her colleagues haven't been reading current educational journals or taken the time to update themselves about new teaching ideas. It is this new teacher's responsibility to introduce her colleagues to books such as Constance Weaver's *Teaching Grammar in Context* (1996) and *Lessons to Share on Teaching Grammar in Context* (1998) and Harry Noden's *Image Grammar: Using Grammatical Structures to Teach Writing* (1999). She may need to become a local expert on grammar pedagogy and teach others about what she knows.

I was in a similar situation years ago regarding my school's use of the research paper as a rote assignment. I realize now that if I hadn't stood up for what I felt was right, I never would have been able to stay at my job as long as I have. I would have become resentful and frustrated. It is also true, however, that speaking up can be a difficult task and might result in isolation from colleagues, who could react defensively and angrily; after all, this teacher is new at the school and does not have the years of experience that many of the other teachers have. So perhaps the best advice is for this teacher to consider her options but to make her final decision about how to suggest modifications in the unit plan based on a thorough analysis of her professional context and the level of resistance to the recommendations for change she expects to confront. At the very least, she can modify the way she approaches grammar and language instruction in her own classes.

A Teacher Responds

I'm impressed with the way this new teacher responded to a difficult situation. I understand her reluctance to make major changes immediately, but I would recommend that she continue to challenge the idea of the isolated and decontextualized grammar unit at the beginning of the school year. Such a unit sends a bad message to the students and teachers in this school: students must "learn" grammar before they are allowed to actually write. This is the way I was taught, and it took me years to get past it. I'm concerned about any pedagogy that forefronts grammar instruction over writing. It also sets up English teachers as grammar experts and creates an atmosphere in which English teachers are expected to correct other people's grammar. I can't even count the number of times someone has said, in response to my telling what I do for a living, "I better watch how I talk." Of course they don't have to watch their language. We all use idiosyncratic speech and writing and speak in home dialects that aren't necessarily "standard." I couldn't imagine reading literature if it were all written only in Standard English. I hope we aren't in a profession that describes writing as grammatical correctness.

Something else this teacher might consider is how she integrates grammar and language instruction into her writing assignments. We don't get much information about this in the narrative—only that she will be teaching minilessons that focus on problems she sees in student writing. This is a good idea, but there are additional ways she can integrate grammar instruction and writing experience. If, for example, she asks students to write memoirs about, as she suggests, "an embarrassing moment," she might require students to include dialogue in the essays. When including this dialogue, students could be encouraged to try reproducing spoken language as they actually hear it in the real world. If a student's essay is about striking out during a baseball game in gym class, perhaps she might include dialogue between the pitcher and the coach, between the other players on her team, or even internal dialogue that captures her thoughts. In preparation for this writing, students could be required to eavesdrop on conversations between people who are similar to those in their memoirs, take notes about what they hear and how they hear it, and then attempt to reproduce these dialectical patterns in their essays. In this way, students could become more aware of dialectical variety, how certain "nonstandard" constructions can be rhetorically powerful, and how such dialects can reflect and affect individual identities and peer relationships.

For Further Discussion

1. What is your opinion of this teacher's approach to grammar? How does it relate to your philosophy of grammar and language instruction?

2. How does the isolated, traditional grammar unit compare to the way you were taught concepts of grammar and language? What do you remember about grammar and language instruction as a middle or high school student? Was this instruction effective for you?

3. How can grammar and language instruction be made productive or relevant? How can it be integrated into the writing process without putting the teacher in the role of enforcer? How might such instruction be used to help students understand the sociopolitical dimensions of language use?

Learning Activities

1. Imagine yourself in a situation similar to this teacher's. Your cooperating teacher for your student teaching, for example, tells you that your first teaching experience with his students will be a grammar unit. What do you do? What are some alternatives you could propose that might be compromise solutions?

2. The first responder to this case mentions teaching the "grammar of different situations." This is an interesting suggestion that places grammar in context and reinforces the fact that grammar "rules" can change depending on the rhetorical situation. Develop a lesson plan that incorporates this approach to grammar instruction.

Language and Grammar Narrative 3

In this story, we see a teacher struggle with the conflict between the realities of her classroom and the theoretical orientation she developed during her teacher education. She uses her experiences and education to strike a compromise and enact a revised and relevant theory of teaching grammar in her English as a second language classroom. This story takes place in a junior high school in a midsize Missouri city.

The New Approach

I took graduate classes at the university that taught me that teaching reading through a whole language approach was the best and most natural way. I agreed, but I found out that sometimes things sound easier to teach than they actually are.

I really felt that my English as a second language (ESL) students needed rules and concrete examples of correct grammar in order to write well in English. But I had two problems with trying to teach grammar through rules and examples: (1) I couldn't explain the rules very well and (2) I had difficulty picking out examples of grammatical constructions in literary texts to discuss with students. Therefore, I decided I had to teach the lessons to my students and learn the rules myself at the same time.

First I read my students' writings in order to identify the grammar errors they made. Then I made a list of the most common errors, using several English grammar books, including Betty Azar's (2002), to find the relevant rule for each error. Next I created a lesson plan for teaching the rules while providing examples. I also adopted a practice that our district was using in the elementary grades to teach error recognition: I wrote a sentence on the board, the students identified the errors within it, and then they explained how to correct the error.

For five years I taught one such grammar lesson each week. On Monday I would present the initial lesson along with a worksheet. On Tuesday, Wednesday, and Thursday, I wrote a sentence on the board that the students had to correct. On Friday I collected and graded the worksheet. Over time the students learned grammar, I learned the rules myself, and as we read stories I began to recognize certain grammar constructions in these texts. Thus, I was getting closer to being able to enact a whole language approach.

Whole language advocates probably wouldn't be completely

▶

happy with my way of teaching grammar, but it was the best way for me to explain to my students why we write the way we do. Now I believe I am ready to teach grammar in a more "whole language" way. Next year I plan to take examples of at least three grammar issues or concepts from a story we read together and that I have identified as problems in students' writing and teach these concepts while we are reading the story. Students will have to find additional examples of the grammar concept or skill in the story. Thus, the grammar lesson will be directly related to the literature that students are reading. Hopefully, in this way I will have solved my dilemma and will be able to teach grammar to second language learners using a whole language approach.

A Teacher Responds

Even though this teacher is a veteran, her dilemma is a common one for newer teachers as they encounter their first classroom and find out that things aren't as they had always imagined them. I understand her decision-making process; often it is much more difficult than expected to translate theoretical concepts into actual classroom practice. But I don't see much of a rationale in her narrative about *why* she makes the decisions she does, other than her own need to become more familiar with grammatical concepts. I'm not denying that what she describes seems to work. I'm betting that students are somewhat attentive and are responding to her methods, but I suspect that the teacher feels obligated to use traditional grammar but doesn't quite know why. I would like to see this teacher ask some hard and reflective questions about why grammar instruction is useful for her second language learners. What does she want such instruction to accomplish? Improved conversational fluency? Improved writing ability? Improved reading comprehension? Or all of the above? Her plans for integrating grammar instruction into literary study seem to be a positive step in this direction. Through this approach, she seems to be consciously trying to enact whole language philosophies when teaching grammar and language skills.

It's important to note that research about teaching writing to second language learners tells us something slightly different from that concerning native English speakers. While it demonstrates that language immersion is effective for second language learners just as it is for native English speakers, and, like a first language, competence in a second language is not most effectively taught through isolated grammatical drills or memorization of terminology, it is also true that grammar instruction plays a different role in the ESL classroom. Clearly, second language writers will have more difficulty with vocabulary, syntax, and idiomatic expressions. They will not have the intuitive "ear" for effective language that many native English speakers have. Therefore, more direct attention may have to be paid to grammar and language instruction and more individual coaching may have to be provided to students. This does not mean, however, that grammar and language should be taught outside the context of a communicative act. On the contrary, research also shows that by engaging in actual reading and writing tasks rather than studying grammar, vocabulary, and usage in isolation, ESL learners can improve their grammatical competence. The NCTE position statement on grammar instruction composed by the Assembly for the Teaching of English Grammar (ATEG, n.d.) provides several ideas for teachers of ESL students, including using sentence "frames" or templates into which students insert words to clarify their part of speech. For more discussion of ESL learners in the English classroom, see Chapter 4.

I encourage this teacher to continue to implement whole language strategies in her ESL curriculum. The results surely will be good.

A Teacher Responds

I respect this teacher for her valiant attempts to integrate whole language strategies when teaching grammar in the ESL classroom. I thought I might take the opportunity presented by this narrative to talk about the concept of "whole language," what it means, and how secondary English teachers can make use of the theory in their classrooms. In general, the theory advocates teaching literacy skills through immersion in "real" texts—books, magazines, visual texts, discussions, etc.—rather than teaching students to read and write using basal readers, worksheets, and narrow phonics-only approaches. One main argument of whole language is that people learn to read by reading, and they learn to write by writing, and that engaging in such authentic experiences is often more helpful and instructive than other kinds of activities. Ken Goodman and Yetta Goodman (K. Goodman, Y. Goodman, & Hood, 1989; K. Goodman, Bird, & Y. Goodman, 1991; Y. Goodman & Wilde, 1992; Y. Goodman, 1996) have been two of the leading authorities on and advocates for whole language in elementary and secondary classrooms. A whole language approach to teaching grammar would involve a connection between grammatical knowledge and authentic reading and writing tasks, such as literary study, as the teacher in this narrative suggests. Her idea about finding examples of grammatical "issues" in books students are reading and then teaching about these issues or concepts within the context of a book is an excellent one.

Next I would like to focus on the problems this teacher identifies: (1) her difficulty explaining "rules" or concepts and (2) her problem with identifying different grammatical issues in the books so that they can be presented for class discussion and analysis. It seems to me that this teacher knows what she would like to do in her class, but she also knows that she is not quite ready to enact the pedagogy she values. So what does she do? She becomes ready. She takes several years to educate not only her students but also herself. She refreshes her knowledge of grammatical concepts and terms and she becomes more comfortable looking at literary texts the students read, with an eye for recognizing interesting grammatical issues that could become topics for discussion. After this preparation, she is ready to jump into a more "pure" whole language approach.

In addition to what this story can teach us about whole language and grammar instruction, I think it says something interesting and important about teacher reflection and education. It's important for teachers to identify both their strengths and their weaknesses and then to take steps to continue to learn and grow. This teacher is an excellent model for younger teachers who are sometimes afraid to admit that they don't know everything. The fact is, no one does, so it's important to be reflective about one's practice and identify areas that can be improved on. Such reflection and growth will be a wonderful benefit to students.

For Further Discussion

1. This teacher believes she had difficulty teaching grammar partly because she could not explain the rules to her students. What do you think English language arts teachers should know about grammar, and what should they be able to explain effectively to students? Why?

2. In a small group, brainstorm ways you might adapt traditional grammar instruction to be consistent with contemporary theory and research that stresses the importance of contextual and whole language approaches to teaching grammar through immersion in reading and writing activities.

3. Think about the similarities and differences between learning a first and a second language. In what ways are both alike? In what ways are they different? To reflect on this question, think about your own experience learning a second language, perhaps in a high school or college class. You might also refer to Chapter 4 for more ideas.

Learning Activities

1. Devise a lesson plan that connects traditional grammar instruction to the study of a specific literary text. As part of this lesson plan, include a rationale for why you believe the lesson will be effective.

2. Write an informal essay about how the social-political aspect of grammar and language use, as well as the concept of Standard English, is relevant to second language learners in the United States. What are some political ideologies often expressed about people speaking languages other than English? What do you think is the purpose of such an ideological stance? How might secondary school ESL students become cognizant of such attitudes in productive, possibly socially active, ways?

Language and Grammar Narrative 4

In this story, a teacher struggles with how to help students become their own editors. She shares her experiences of trying to teach grammar in context but finding that students still seem to view her instruction as decontextualized and therefore rarely apply what she has taught to their own writing. This narrative takes place in a rural high school of about three hundred students in central Missouri.

Why Do I Bother? Teaching Minilessons to Student Writers

I graduated from college with my teaching certification in 1989; therefore, I had been exposed to many contemporary theoretical approaches to teaching grammar, including the importance of teaching it within the context of student writing. I believed in this approach, and it made perfect sense to me when I was an undergraduate in methods courses. When I started teaching a high school composition class, however, I struggled with the concept. I taught minilessons to my students on issues such as sentence fragments, run-ons, parallel structure, and comma use, all grammar and editing problems that I had identified (and marked) time and time again in their essays. I would notice, for example, that five out of fifteen students had written more than five sentence fragments as they completed an expository essay assignment. Therefore, dutifully, I would pull out my sentence fragment worksheets and exercises, copy them, and review the concept with my students. I noticed two problems. First, the so-called minilesson would often stretch much longer than the intended ten

▶

minutes of instruction. It would end up taking students a long time to fill out the worksheets, and the grammar lesson could take up almost the entire period. Second, even if students seemed to understand the concept when they filled out the worksheets and answered in-class questions, I would inevitably see the *same error* in their next set of papers. In other words, there seemed to be little transfer between the exercises and real writing tasks.

I didn't know what to do. Why were my minilessons not working when they worked so well for Nancie Atwell? What was I doing wrong? And I also struggled with a related problem concerning grammar and mechanics—I would meticulously mark errors on student drafts, only to have students correct what I marked and *only* what I marked. They didn't seem to see or recognize errors on their own and would become angry when I counted off for these errors because I hadn't, they said, told them the errors existed. I wanted my students to read their own papers closely and begin to edit themselves, applying what I was teaching during those minilessons. But it just never seemed to happen that way.

A Teacher Responds

This problem is very common among teachers, and this teacher's question is one that deserves a thoughtful response. First, I will say that I know exactly what she is talking about. I have had similar experiences in my own classroom. It does seem to be a particularly frustrating dilemma, especially when we are trying to teach as we have been taught to do and things still don't seem to be working. I commend this teacher for trying to teach grammar in context and for trying to approach grammatical instruction through a series of short lessons instead of lengthy units. But I have a couple of suggestions that might help.

First, I'm wondering about the use of the long worksheets. One of the problems she notes is that her minilessons often turn into period-long lessons. When this happens, the students might be losing intellectual contact with whatever piece of writing they are working on. Even though the teacher may have chosen the exercises based on problems she identified in their writing, the students may not see that connection at all. Perhaps the teacher could use examples from students' own writing (with the students' permission, of course) so that the "error" is inherently connected to their current writing task. Or perhaps the teacher could write the paper herself, purposely engaging in several "errors" that she could then ask students to correct in class. Also, I think she should try hard to make the minilesson truly "mini" and take up only ten to fifteen minutes of class time. Then students can transition back into their writing task and maybe begin to understand, even unconsciously, that grammar and mechanics are intrinsically related to writing tasks.

Second, I think it's important for this teacher to remember that even minilessons can be taught as decontextualized exercises if they aren't approached rhetorically. Any instruction in grammar, mechanics, or usage should be surrounded by the discourse of audience, purpose, and effect. In other words, when the teacher is reviewing the sentence fragment issue, perhaps she should do more than tell students that writing a sentence fragment is "wrong." Perhaps she should also tell them that most of the time it is considered incorrect because it is an incomplete thought and is therefore confusing or unclear to the reader. Or even tell students that sometimes authors actually choose to write fragments to elicit a certain stylistic effect or emphasize a point. In this way, the concept of the sentence fragment is not seen as simply a rule not to be broken but instead is understood as connected to communicative tasks and rhetorical principles. I can't say that these approaches will solve this teacher's problems altogether, but I do believe that if she practices them consistently over time she might well see a change in her students' behavior.

A Teacher Responds

I would like to respond to a specific part of the problem this teacher describes, a problem she alludes to only briefly at the end of her story. This is the issue of marking student errors and then having students who only correct things based on the teacher's commentary. This is a problem with which many English teachers struggle. We are, for the most part, a hard-working and caring bunch of people, so we want to help students be the best writers they can be. Therefore, our sincere desire for student achievement often translates into obsessive or excessive marking on student papers in which we note every single grammar, punctuation, and spelling error we can find. We think this is helpful, and in many ways it certainly is. It is simple for a student writer to then go back and "fix" everything we noted. What many teachers don't recognize, however, is that by doing this obsessive marking we are teaching students to be dependent on us, or some other outside reader, forever. Instead of teaching students that in order to be successful writers they always need to have a competent editor read behind them, we should try to help students become their own internal editors who eventually are able to proofread their own papers and detect and correct errors themselves. We can begin to do this by minimizing the number of marks we make on student papers, perhaps limiting ourselves to noting a single *type* of error per draft.

This is not to say that I don't value peer editing or workshopping activities. Anyone who has ever written anything of significance knows that an outside reader can be essential both for editing and for responding to content. But I'm not sure English teachers always point out the difference between understanding writing as an inherently social act and therefore dependent on reader responses and completely giving up a sense of self-efficacy as a writer. Additionally, students will be unable to make the connection between grammar, mechanics, and effective communication if they are always correcting based on what a teacher, or a peer, tells them is right. This approach to editing simply reinforces grammar as something that is simply right or wrong and learned through rote memorization.

One other point in response to this teacher has to do with the connection between *reading* and grammar. In the January 2003 issue of *English Journal*, a teacher named Paul E. Doniger wrote an article titled "Language Matters: Grammar as a Tool in the Teaching of Literature." In this essay, Doniger argues that an analysis of the grammatical choices an author makes can help readers interpret and understand literary texts. It seems to me that if a teacher practices such an approach when teaching literature, then when students write their own texts they will have a richer understanding of how grammatical choices can affect the style, tone, meaning, and effectiveness of a piece of writing.

For Further Discussion

1. What do you think is the purpose of a minilesson? Why do certain teachers and theorists recommend them for grammar instruction? Do you agree with this type of approach? Why or why not?

2. Thinking back to Chapter 2, "Narratives about Teaching Writing," what were some of the suggestions given for responding to student work in progress? How do these suggestions correspond to the theories of teaching grammar discussed in this chapter?

3. Do you think there's any connection between teaching grammar and language and teaching literature? If so, what is it? If not, why not?

Learning Activities

1. Think about a writing assignment you completed in middle or high school. How was grammar instruction incorporated into this assignment? How was grammatical correctness assessed? Do you think the instruction was effective? Why or why not?

2. In a small group, create two different and specific plans for responding to student writing. These plans should not be rubrics but descriptions of how you will approach such response philosophically. You may want to vary plans according to the genre of writing to which you are responding, the purpose given to students for writing it, and the intended audience.

In Closing

We have often heard teachers ask questions such as "Am I ignoring grammar?" or "Am I focusing on grammar too much?" The teaching of grammar and language can often be difficult, since many of us were taught grammatical concepts in traditional ways, such as through decontextualized sentence diagramming or handbook exercises. We have found that English teachers often enjoyed grammar in school and therefore expect that their students will share their interest. Only later do they understand that their experience with grammar was often unique and not shared by many of their peers.

We believe in approaching grammar primarily within the context of student writing and reading. We also believe that the exploration of social and political dimensions of language should be an integral part of an English language arts curriculum because such study further contextualizes language study and increases students' perceptions of its relevance. NCTE's Assembly for the Teaching of English Grammar (ATEG, n.d.) created a position statement on the teaching of grammar that is posted on the NCTE Web site. This statement begins by arguing, "Grammar is important because it is the language that makes it possible for us to talk about language. . . . [K]*nowing about* grammar also helps us understand what makes sentences and paragraphs clear and interesting and precise."

ATEG's position on grammar is that it is necessary; like us, however, they believe that it should be taught within a meaningful rhetorical context. We do not believe that teachers should ignore grammar instruction in their classrooms. It's too easy to say that grammar should never be taught. On the contrary, it's how you choose to teach it that is important.

As we finish this discussion, consider the following questions as you plan how to bring grammar into your classroom and develop a philosophy of teaching language and grammar to secondary students:

1. Do I approach grammar productively (in ways that students can use to improve their own writing, reading, and speaking)?

2. Do I make the complexity and contextuality of grammar clear, or am I simply teaching Standard English without considering other English dialects or rhetorical concepts?

3. Are my discussions of grammar empowering my students to become better writers and communicators or simply making them fearful of experimenting with language?

Additional Texts and Resources about Teaching Language and Grammar

Books

Haussamen, Brock, with Amy Benjamin, Martha Kolln, Rebecca S. Wheeler, and members of NCTE's Assembly for the Teaching of English Grammar. Urbana, IL: National Council of Teachers of English.

> NCTE's Assembly for the Teaching of English Grammar provides this much-needed resource for K–12 teachers who wonder what to do about grammar—how to teach it, how to apply it, how to learn what they themselves were never taught. It offers teachers ways to negotiate the often conflicting goals of testing, confident writing, the culturally inclusive classroom, and the teaching of Standard English while also honoring other varieties of English. This hands-on approach to grammar in the classroom includes numerous examples and practical vignettes describing real teachers' classroom experiences with specific grammar lessons—including ESL issues—as well as a review of grammar basics.

Noguchi, Rei R. (1991). *Grammar and the Teaching of Writing: Limits and Possibilities.* Urbana, IL: National Council of Teachers of English.

> Noguchi takes a practical look at how grammar can be taught in the writing classroom to minimize reliance on terminology and maximize the positive effects on student writing. This often-cited text covers a lot of ground in a straightforward, readable fashion as Noguchi provides an overview of research in grammar instruction and explores the pedagogical implications. This is a great book for the beginning teacher.

Shaughnessy, Mina P. (1977). *Errors and Expectations: A Guide for the Teacher of Basic Writing.* New York: Oxford University Press.

> This book is a classic among composition teachers at the secondary and postsecondary levels. Shaughnessy explains how student errors in grammar and language actually have a logic that once understood can help teachers teach academic writing without condescension or classism.

Strong, William. (1994). *Sentence Combining: A Composing Book* (3rd ed.). New York: McGraw-Hill.

> Strong, a noted expert on sentence combining, explains the practice and provides several innovative and classroom-tested exercises for students. This text is both a theoretical overview and a compilation of concrete ideas for sentence-combining assignments.

Weaver, Constance. (1979). *Grammar for Teachers: Perspectives and Definitions.* Urbana, IL: National Council of Teachers of English.

> In this book, Weaver defines many grammatical issues and concepts within a practical and pedagogical context. She includes in-depth discussion of the connection between grammar and the reading and writing processes.

Electronic Resources

The NCTE Assembly for the Teaching of English Grammar
www.ateg.org/

> The ATEG site offers a series of resources including questions and answers about teaching grammar, tips for teaching grammar, an extensive bibliography of grammar teaching, and other resources of interest to English language arts teachers.

NCTE Solutions Center Grammar Section
www.ncte.org/solutions/grammar.shtml

> This site archives several NCTE position statements and resolutions on grammar as well as several "starter sheets" and a link to the NCTE Assembly for the Teaching of English Grammar.

Purdue University Online Writing Lab (OWL) Grammar Section
http://owl.english.purdue.edu/handouts/grammar/index.html

> Of the online grammar handbooks available, we find this site to be the best developed and theoretically sound, placing grammatical skills within the context of writing and offering strong re-

sources to students on most grammatical issues. This is a good site on which to find handouts for minilessons or for individual student help.

4 Narratives about Teaching Second Language Learners in the English Class

C hildren who come from non-English-speaking homes constitute the fastest growing population of school-age children in the United States. According to Marguerite Ann Snow (2000), the number of limited English proficient (LEP) students increased 109 percent from 1985 to 1995, and estimates were that by the year 2000 the majority of students in fifty or more U.S. cities would come from language minority backgrounds (p. v). Limited English proficient is a term used by the U.S. government for students identified as having a home language other than English and who need additional instruction to be able to successfully take classes in English. In Indiana, where one of us is a teacher educator, the Indiana Department of Education Web site reports that in 2000–2001 there were 212 different languages spoken in K–12 classrooms across the state (Spanish being the most common) and 17,194 LEP students. As a consequence of these increased numbers, English as a second language (ESL) students, sometimes referred to as English to speakers of other languages (ESOL) students, make up a larger percentage of students in our English language arts classes.

While ESL students often enroll in "regular" content area classes, many secondary schools also have ESL programs that approach instruction of second language learners in a variety of ways, including transitional bilingual programs, "pull out" ESL classrooms, and "sheltered" English instruction programs (all of which are explained in more detail later in this chapter). Although many schools have strong ESL programs, many other schools are struggling to meet the needs of a growing ESL student population in the face of overwhelming obstacles, including a lack of qualified bilingual and ESL teachers, ideological opposition to bilingual instruction by conservative political groups, and minimal resources devoted to second language learning. Because of these and other obstacles, ESL learners often receive only one to three years of ESL instruction before being mainstreamed into regular content courses, even though research has shown that it could take students from four to ten years of study to become proficient in academic English regardless of their fluency in conversational English (Echevarria, Vogt, & Short, 2000, p. 5).

English classrooms can provide the most challenges for ESL students because they are asked not only to use the language effectively but also to speak and write in complex ways about literary texts written in English. Compounding the problem is that English teachers often are not educated in second language English instruction, and therefore they can find it difficult to meet the needs of second language learners in their classes. They were educated primarily to teach English as a content area "subject," an education that consists primarily of instruction in reading and analyzing literature and composing texts in various academic genres; they were not taught how second language learners may approach the regular content of the English class differently, nor were they always exposed to theories of language learning and development. Jana Echevarria, Mary Ellen Vogt, and Deborah Short (2000) write, "Most teacher preparation colleges do not provide undergraduates with strategies for teaching linguistically and culturally diverse students," and while teachers in areas where there are more second language learners (the western and southern United States) tend to have received more university preparation, most content area teachers remain essentially unprepared and receive little information or help in university course work or in inservice workshops (p. 4).

It is difficult to talk about second language education without including a discussion of political issues that often affect the work of ESL professionals. Teachers of English to Speakers of Other Languages (TESOL) is a professional organization of educators interested in K–adult second language learning (the acronym also often refers to the field of second language education itself). In 1987, TESOL passed a language rights resolution supporting measures that protect the right of all individuals to preserve and foster their linguistic and cultural origins and opposing all measures declaring English the official language of the United States. James W. Tollefson (2002) writes that language policies in education are "an important mechanism by which states manage social and political control" (p. 5). Language conflicts often have their root in fear and insecurity over economic and nationalistic issues, and consequently they can elicit high emotion, defensiveness, and anger. When U.S. politicians (and often U.S. citizens) insist that "every American should speak English," or that different languages lead to a divisive culture and a lack of national loyalty, it is clear that language policy and ideology are often closely linked, which often makes language battles difficult to fight. Sonntag and Pool (1987) showed that

Most Americans (whether or not they support special services for linguistic minorities) share many assumptions about language, including for example the validity of competence in English as an indicator of national loyalty, the presumed neutrality of Standard English, and the sufficiency of willpower for its mastery. (qtd. in McGroarty, 2002, p. 20)

Therefore, educators must be ready to support fair and pluralistic language policies that often fly in the face of conservative politics. But we do not want to imply that having ESL students in the "regular" English classroom is a thing to be dreaded or a surefire way to draw community criticism. ESL students can add much to a class by introducing American students to linguistic and cultural differences about which they were previously unaware.

What Is *Good* Language Arts Instruction for ESL Students?

What are some basics of effective ESL instruction in the secondary English classroom? Before we describe different pedagogical strategies that can be effective in mainstream English classes for second language learners, we want to review some of the major curricular approaches to ESL that frame these strategies. TESOL has established three broad goals for ESL learners of all ages, goals that include personal, social, and academic uses of English. Each goal is subsequently associated with three distinct standards that can lead to English proficiency:

> **Goal 1:** Use English to communicate in social settings.
>
> **Goal 2:** Use English to achieve academically in all content areas.
>
> **Goal 3:** Use English in socially and culturally appropriate ways. (TESOL, 1997, p. 9)

The development of these goals and standards in 1997 was a milestone in ESL teacher education because they set clear and consistent educational priorities for ESL programs that are often conducted in radically different ways from school to school and from state to state. A complete list of the goals and standards is available in book form from TESOL and also online at www.tesol.org/. The standards, while written primarily for second language or bilingual teachers, can also be helpful to content area teachers who may have little knowledge of the needs of ESL students or what research has demonstrated about effective ESL instruction.

To clarify, ESL instruction is somewhat different from bilingual education. In bilingual education, students are initially taught in both

English and their native language. The native language is used for academic instruction so that students do not get behind in content area learning while they are learning English. ESL instruction, on the other hand, focuses on teaching students English using a variety of instructional strategies, such as simplified or sheltered English, gestures, and pictures, to convey academic content. Many teachers in ESL classrooms (or in content area classrooms into which ESL students are mainstreamed) do not speak the home languages evidenced in their classrooms; therefore, it would be impossible for them to instruct the students in their native languages.

The following list summarizes major ESL program types in the United States and their strengths and weaknesses based on the research of Baker (1996), Diaz-Rico and Weed (1995), Faltis and Hudelson (1998), and Ovando and Collier (1998):

1. **"Sink or Swim" Programs.** These programs are sometimes called "submersion" programs because they place non-English-speaking students in mainstream English language classrooms without any special support. Most ESL professionals consider this model an inadequate form of instruction for English learners (Berman et al., 1992; Ramirez, 1992; Thomas & Collier, 1995). Incidentally, the sink-or-swim approach was ruled illegal in 1974 by the U.S. Supreme Court in *Lau v. Nichols.* The judge in this case ruled that Chinese students in San Francisco were being unfairly treated when they were not given any explicit English instruction.

2. **"Pull Out" ESL Programs.** These programs are often combined with submersion programs, providing ESL students a minimum amount of English instruction during the school day (as little as twenty minutes or as much as several hours of instruction). This format is usually considered the second weakest model of instruction for second language learners.

3. **Transitional Bilingual Education.** This type of program is currently the most common in U.S. secondary schools. This model is sometimes called the "early exit" transitional model, and the goal is to provide first language instruction only while children are learning English. Then students are moved into mainstream classrooms within two to three years, and the first language instruction stops. According to Ovando and Collier (1998), the transitional model has many problems. First, research has shown that two to three years of first language instruction is too little (Collier, 1995), and second, transitional classes are often stigmatized as being remedial or for "slow" students (p. 57).

4. "Late Exit" Transitional Programs. ESL educators generally prefer late-exit programs because research shows that students enrolled in such programs at least through the fourth grade achieve more academic success (Berman et al., 1992; Ovando & Collier, 1998; Ramirez, Yuen, Ramey, & Pasta, 1991; Thomas & Collier, 1995). Late-exit programs are also called "maintenance" or "developmental" bilingual programs because they develop the first language (L1) over time while adding English (L2). These programs have "as a major goal the development of proficiency in both the learner's L1 *and* in English, and the utilization of both languages in the learning of significant content" (Faltis & Hudelson, 1998, p. 30; emphasis added).

Diaz-Rico and Weed (1995) characterize maintenance programs as demonstrating an empowering view of schooling for second language learners because they enable ESL students to achieve in content courses at a level comparable to their English-speaking peers while simultaneously learning a second language. Instead of seeking to "take away" the native language (and often culture), the program strives to "add on" a second language. Such an approach is supported by research. A four-year longitudinal study of two thousand Spanish-speaking students in five states found that late-exit bilingual programs proved superior to early-exit bilingual and English-only immersion programs (Ramirez et al., 1991).

5. Immersion Education. This model is often seen as an enrichment model, but it is often misused and misunderstood in the United States. Immersion programs, begun in St. Lambert, Quebec, Canada, in the 1960s, immersed children from majority language and cultural backgrounds (i.e., English) in a minority language (i.e., French). The objective was to produce bilingual and biliterate individuals who would become more tolerant of their minority-culture peers. The success of this program, however, is often touted by English-only advocates in the United States as proof that total submersion in a second language without first language instruction is educationally effective. What they forget is that the Canadian students who were immersed were the language *majority* students (as opposed to the language *minority* ones), and the goal was cultural growth, not content area education. Additionally, in the Canadian model there was no ethnocentric threat of replacing a home language or culture with a new one.

6. Structured Immersion. According to Ovando and Collier (1998), this is a "misnamed program model that was promoted by English only proponents with a political agenda in the early 1980s" (p. 56). It was approved by ballot initiative in the state of California in June 1998 through what was called Proposition 227. A controversial aspect of this model is that LEP students receive English instruction for usually no more than one year (Proposition 227 stipulates one year) and have little or no first language instruction during this time. After the year is up, students are placed in classes with native-English-speaking students and are expected to assimilate completely. Many ESL educators believe that structured immersion is a misapplication of the Canadian enrichment model discussed in item 5 (Hernandez-Chavez, 1984).

When you think about your philosophy of teaching English language arts, you should not overlook the needs of second language learners. Whether or not you are bilingual or have any education in second language learning, this is an issue you must consider, as the statistics quoted at the beginning of this chapter demonstrate. To help you think about pedagogical strategies that can help second language learners in the English classroom, we provide a list of approaches that we consider examples of best practices in teaching second language learners in the English language arts classroom. If you want to learn more about any of these approaches, see the annotated bibliography at the end of the chapter for sources to consult.

Characteristics of Effective Second Language Pedagogy in English Classrooms

1. Recognize That Academic English and Conversational English Are Not Always the Same. Often those advocating submersion approaches to second language instruction assume that once a student can speak English conversationally or socially he or she can also function successfully in an academic classroom. Sometimes this may be true; however, a content area classroom uses vocabulary and communicative and discursive methods that are very different from social conversation. Consequently, ESL students may need continued instruction in English as it is used in various academic settings and contexts long after they are proficient conversationalists.

2. Make Language Visible. ESL students can often be assisted in content area classes through visual representations, gestures, and facial expressions used by teachers to supplement instruction and reinforce their points. This "visual" approach is part of what is termed the *sheltered English* approach to ESL instruction. Sheltered English, or specially designed academic instruction in English (SDAIE), consists of content or academic instruction in English organized to promote second language acquisition as well as content knowledge acquisition. A sheltered approach usually means that teachers adjust speech, paraphrase, give examples, provide analogies, elaborate on student responses, promote class discussions, and adjust tasks so that they are incrementally challenging. Visual aids, modeling, graphic organizers, predictions, adapted texts, cooperative learning, peer tutoring, multicultural content, and native language support are also utilized (Echevarria, Vogt, & Short, 2000, p. 9). At its best, the sheltered approach allows for content learning, English language learning, and social integration into "regular" classes. It does not mean talking down to students or simplifying content.

3. Recognize That the Problems ESL Students Have with Reading and Writing Are Similar to the Problems of Native English Speakers. Much current research confirms the similarity of writing and reading processes for both first and second language writers (Ammon, 1985; Edelsky, 1981, 1982). Second language educators value the process approach to writing and find it effective for second language learners. Additionally, researchers believe that the reading process is fundamentally the same process of construction of meaning across languages (Goodman & Goodman, 1978; Hudelson, 1981). Miscue analysis research carried out with adolescent ESL learners found that these learners worked to construct meaning as they read texts in their new language in ways similar to native English speakers. Consequently, many of the same English language arts best practices for native English speakers are recommended for second language learners; for example, reading texts about familiar topics and themes, participating in literature and writing discussion groups, and process writing approaches are useful strategies for second language learners.

4. At the Same Time, Recognize That There Are Differences between ESL Students and Native-English-Speaking Students. Even though ESL and native-English-speaking students share many of the same struggles and benefit from many of the same strategies in the English classroom, second language learners may need to have some adjustments made in the way these strategies are implemented. When using the process approach to writing with ESL students, for example, teachers may need to slow down the process and allow more opportunities for conferencing and workshopping. Tony Silva's (1993) meta-analysis of research in second language writing describes how research has shown L2 writing to be distinct from L1 writing. The composing processes of second language writers was less fluent, more difficult, less effective, took longer, and was less complex than that of native English writers (pp. 657–75). To overcome these difficulties, teachers should pay particular attention to the ESL writer's needs and implement necessary pedagogical modifications. ESL students might benefit, for example, from writing more about topics they are familiar with since such a context often provides increased knowledge of vocabulary. Similarly, ESL student readers might benefit from teachers choosing texts for reading that are about topics with which students are familiar. By providing reading material on content familiar to students and/or by building background knowledge prior to reading a text, teachers can offset reading comprehension difficulties (Peregoy & Boyle, 2001, p. 261). One good example of such a text might be created through the "language experience" approach, whereby students dictate in English stories they know and the teacher or a peer writes these stories down, creating texts that later serve as the basis for reading instruction. For the ESL student, reading takes on greater significance because it not only provides content for thought and discussion but also provides a model for an English text.

5. Understand That Students' First Languages Should Not Be Ignored or Banished from Classroom Use. It is important that a student's first language be welcomed in an educational setting as the student learns English. For many reasons, it is not useful or effective to banish the student's home language from the classroom: (1) teachers should encourage students' parents (who may not be bilingual) to participate in the education of their children; (2) language is often associated with culture, and teachers must not run the risk of encouraging students to reject their home culture along with their home language; and (3) first languages are often essential for effective subject or content learning as students learn English. Culturally responsive teaching (Bartolome, 1994) that is sensitive to diverse ways of learning, behaving, and using language is essential to the effective ESL classroom. In addition, teachers can build on the strengths of ESL students and encourage them to share their diverse knowledge and experiences with their classmates.

6. Use Thematic Instruction and Collaborative Activities. Theme-based instruction is useful for ESL students because it can create a meaningful conceptual framework for learning new content that can help students with limited English vocabulary and with few experiences with academic English. Just as with native-English-speaking students, thematic units can create interest, motivation, a sense of involvement, and an understanding of purpose. Additionally, teachers can facilitate peer support of ESL students by creating classroom activities that allow them to use their home language in interactions with their native-English-speaking peers both for purposes of learning correct English and for sharing their cultural experiences and knowledge.

7. Develop Working Knowledge about Theories of Language Acquisition. Although these theories are primarily about first language acquisition, they can be applied to second language learning in useful ways. Teachers should have a working knowledge of the research and theories of linguists such as Noam Chomsky (1957), B. F. Skinner (1957) and M. A. K. Halliday (1994), as well as theorists of second language acquisition such as Stephen Krashen (1982). As much as possible, English teachers should be aware of past and current trends in language acquisition research, including more current approaches that emphasize the social, contextual, and political nature of language acquisition.

8. Advocate for the English Language Learners in Your School and Community. Education is political, and language and literacy education seems even more political than education in other content areas. As we stated in the introduction to this chapter, language laws and related educational policies about language teaching often have as much to do with political ideologies as with pedagogical theories. Recently, standardized tests have become more popular and common in public schools in response to President George W. Bush's 2001 educational plan called "No Child Left Behind," which endorses the state and nationwide testing of educational standards as a way to improve student learning. As teachers of ESL students, it is important that we recognize the special problems such tests raise for second language learners. In some states, there are currently no special provisions made for second language students taking high-stakes standardized tests; this may be changing, however, as educators and politicians recognize that second-language-speaking students should be tested in the language that will ensure the most accurate assessment of content knowledge. When ESL students fail state-mandated tests (and then sometimes fail to graduate from high school), it is often due, at least in part, to their lack of language skills. It is hard to answer a question correctly when you do not understand the language in which it is written.

9. Recognize and Reject Myths about Second Language Learning. The ESL standards book (TESOL, 1997) identifies three myths about second language learning: (1) ESL students learn English easily and quickly simply by being exposed to and surrounded by native speakers; (2) when

ESL learners are able to converse comfortably in English, they have developed proficiency in the language; and (3) in earlier times, immigrant children learned English rapidly and assimilated easily into American life (p. 3). Recognizing these statements as myths is important to beginning to understand the goals of ESL instruction as well as the ideologies and political agendas that drive much educational policy in the United States.

Controversies in ESL Instruction

1. Additive Bilingualism versus Subtractive Bilingualism. *Additive bilingualism* is the name of the educational approach that views the addition of second language abilities as concurrent with continued development of primary language abilities, including reading and writing. *Subtractive bilingualism* refers to the belief that when an individual develops a second language fully it means the eventual loss of the primary language and, by association, the related culture.

2. "Sink or Swim" versus Various Types of Educational Support. Some educators and political leaders advocate a total submersion program (sink or swim) that places students in regular classes without any (or very little) first language instruction or other special language support. Research has shown that this approach is likely to result in failure, and many of us would agree that it seems unethical. In support of educational support for second language learners, Congress passed Title VII of the Elementary and Secondary Education Act in 1968, creating and providing funding for bilingual education programs (Peregoy & Boyle, 2001, p. 19). In 1974 the U.S. Supreme Court ruled in the *Lau* decision that the San Francisco schools had discriminated against Chinese students by not providing them with any first language support or second language instruction. In 1975 the Office of Civil Rights issued guidelines that held school districts accountable for the special language needs of language minority children who are non-English-speaking or have limited English proficiency (Walling, 1993, p. 15).

3. English-Only Movements versus Language Pluralism. English-only legislation (such as ballot initiatives like California's 1998 Proposition 227) is a manifestation of the belief that language is linked to culture and that cultural difference can create national disharmony and political division. Proposition 227 passed on June 2, 1998, and while it was temporarily blocked by lawsuits, it has since gone into effect. The law outlaws "nearly all classes taught in languages besides English and replace[s] them with an English language class lasting one school year" (Asimov, 1998). At the time of the law's passage, California had 1.4 million non-English-speaking students in its schools, or nearly one in four students. Many believe such laws are discriminatory against speakers of other languages in the United States and that they promote an attitude of ethnocentrism and aggressive monoculturalism that stifles diversity. In order to confront and defeat such initiatives, professional educators and researchers must be able to articulate the goals of ESL and bilingual instruction clearly and effectively.

Narratives

In this chapter, we present four stories that focus on the teaching of English to second language learners. Classroom teachers who have taught second language students either in ESL classes or in "regular" English language arts classes tell these stories, and they demonstrate many of the practices and controversies outlined above.

The first narrative, "A Laughable Moment of Understanding," tells the story of how humor can demonstrate English language proficiency as well as cultural knowledge while lightening the classroom atmosphere. The second story, "How Do We Make Language Learning Stick?," focuses on one student who spends time completing workbook drills in an effort to learn English but who ultimately fails to gain much English language proficiency. The third narrative, "ESL Students and the Loss of Cultural Identity," tells the story of a team of eighth-grade teachers who used the young adult novel *Julie of the Wolves* by Jean Craighead George as a way to encourage ESL students to think and write about the difficulties inherent in adjusting to new cultural surroundings. The last story, "Dictionary Use and Language Learning," describes problems that may arise when second language learners in high school rely on dual-language dictionaries to complete course assignments.

ESL Narrative 1

The following story shows how the expression of humor can be one way ESL students demonstrate knowledge of English language and American culture. The narrative also describes a classroom using collaboration and peer interaction to facilitate English language learning. This teacher teaches ESL classes in a suburban school in north central Missouri.

A Laughable Moment of Understanding

Sometimes, in the middle of a lesson, laughter may occur. Throughout my years of teaching, I've noticed that when an ESL student can express a statement that makes listeners or readers laugh, that student shows a greater comprehension of the situation and is making schematic connections. For instance, just this spring one of my students showed a real sense of humor while communicating in English.

I had one sheltered science class for beginning ESL students. This class consisted of eight students from various continents and countries: Mexico, Russia, Sudan, Bosnia, and Korea. Some of them were not verbalizing in English; some were verbalizing a little bit. These were eighth- and ninth-grade students attending a junior high school in a midwestern city containing three colleges, one being the University of Missouri. These eight students and I were discussing the term *species* one day. In the past, I've known ESL students to have a difficult time understanding this term; therefore, I was trying to ask questions to help support their learning. The nine of us were gathered around a small, rectangular table, each holding a picture of the one endangered animal we had chosen to research and give a PowerPoint presentation on.

We started with Karina. "Which species did you select?" I asked.

"I selected the tiger," she answered.

"Is there only one type of tiger?" I asked.

"Oh, no," she said emphatically. "There are a few other kinds of tigers."

"What are they?"

"Well, there's the Russian tiger, the white tiger, and—I don't know," Karina said as she ran out of ideas.

We were all quiet, thinking.

I asked again, "Are there any other types of tigers anyone can think of?"

"Well, of course," Omama said exuberantly. "There's the Mizzou Tiger."

We all broke into laughter, knowing full well that this tiger is just a mascot for the University of Missouri football team. And Omama knew this as well, since her father worked at the university. Even though half the students had just come to Columbia, they were already acquainted with the Tiger symbol and its special meaning in the city. That day, Omama showed an understanding of our conversation and the local culture through humor, demonstrating greater comprehension of the English language than I had realized she possessed.

A Teacher Responds

I love this story because it narrates success in the ESL classroom and shows students interacting and having fun. Collaborative learning is important in the ESL class as students struggle to be comfortable in a new culture as well as learn to speak the language. The teacher's strategy of questioning students in a group for examples when they are learning a new concept or vocabulary word is a good one. She enabled them to learn from one another in addition to learning from her. The teacher says that she is teaching in an ESL class using a "sheltered" approach, which means that she is supplementing content area learning (in this case science) with visual aids, clarifying language, additional examples, and other supplementary materials and methods. The teacher mentions using PowerPoint presentations as part of an assignment, and this is another good example of the sheltered approach, as well as an interactive, hands-on way for students to learn.

I believe that humor often is an expression of a sophisticated understanding of language. In the case of Omama, her humor demonstrates both her understanding of the word *tiger* and her integration into the culture of her new community. If the teacher had not allowed her students the opportunity to interact and talk with one another, this opportunity for humor and for making a thoughtful, even clever, joke might never have existed. On further thought, perhaps Omama's joke did even more than *demonstrate* her understanding of English and her new culture; perhaps sharing this play on words also allowed her to *stretch* her understanding a bit. To be able to make a joke that depends on the dual meaning of a word, a student must engage in relatively sophisticated thinking about language, and the very act of mentally forming and then telling the joke to others could be evidence of such complex linguistic thought. Additionally, Omama's joke may also have helped her peers progress in their understanding of English as they listened to and deconstructed the humor in Omama's statement.

Humor can be useful in the secondary English classroom, both when the teacher is teaching native English speakers and when he or she is teaching students who are learning English as a foreign language. Unfortunately, laughing and joking in the classroom are often perceived as disruptive behavior, and of course sometimes they *can* be inappropriate (e.g., mocking or making fun). But humor can bring people together by establishing a sense of community or a feeling of collegiality, and it is a creative, sophisticated expression of discourse. Through humor, students can begin to understand language use (and education) as potentially playful and even fun.

A Teacher Responds

This story reminds me of an experience I had with a group of six seventh- and eighth-grade Japanese ESL students. Because our class was their ESL/English class, my students and I read many pieces of literature (in simplified text versions) and wrote response papers. In addition, during each daily forty-five-minute class session, we spent ten to fifteen minutes reviewing content assignments for their social studies, science, and health classes. Although my students never made errors similar to Omama's play on words, they frequently made mistakes with language, often imposing on English what they knew innately about their native language structures. These errors came up in writing pieces or in class discussions. When we discussed these errors and corrected them, there was often hysterical laughter, not at any one student but at the silliness of how this error occurred.

One day after having made one of these mixed-up word errors, Manami, an eighth grader, said, "Mrs. O., I think I'm speaking Japanglish!" Of course, everyone in the group chimed in that they spoke Japanglish, too.

I said, "You know what would be fun to do? Let's create our own Japanglish dictionary. But in it we could also put the correct words we meant to use. What do you think?"

Out of this silly moment, our Japanglish dictionary was born, complete with illustrations and corrections in appropriate English. Throughout the entire school year, we added new words and the real ones we were trying to use. In fact, when errors occurred in other classes, the students brought those words back to the ESL class for discussion and correction. The students illustrated their errors in cartoon fashion right in the book.

Humor provided my students a way to deal with the stress of developing English language skills. It alleviated the fears of making errors and feeling foolish in front of their peers. It also made language learning, and vocabulary in particular, stick. We would never forget the "Japanglish" errors. They were the most fun.

For Further Discussion

1. Think of a joke you've heard recently or one that you simply remember. What emotional level does it appeal to (from early grade school up)? What thinking or knowledge does it assume or validate?

2. Do you think that humor differs across cultures? If so, how might the teacher of ESL students approach humor in the classroom differently than the teacher of American students whose first language is English?

3. Can you think of any literary texts you've read that contain humor and could prompt a discussion of the rhetorical effects of humor? Which ones? Why?

Learning Activities

1. Create a writing or speaking assignment that requires students to use humor. Examples include puns, jokes, tall tales, and skits.

2. In collaborative groups, brainstorm ways you could bring the community into your classroom (e.g., celebration of ethnic holidays, field trips, discussion of local politics, etc.). Brainstorm a list of possible assignments or projects that incorporate community issues, events, icons, or priorities to teach English language arts concepts or skills.

ESL Narrative 2

Many times language learning is understood as memorization and recitation, and workbook exercises can lend themselves to this type of approach. When only memorization and recitation are called on as pedagogical strategies, however, many important aspects of effective second language learning are ignored, such as the need to make the new language relevant to students by providing a meaningful context and using the first language as a bridge to eventual content area instruction in English. This English and Spanish teacher tells the story of one student in a northwestern Indiana school who seems to want to learn English but for whom a textbook-driven approach is not working.

How Do We Make Language Learning Stick?

When Jorge entered my classroom, he had been attending our school for one semester after moving here from Puerto Rico, and he had been working during one class period with an English- and Spanish-speaking part-time tutor. He was taking five regular classes (earth science, math, English 9, Spanish 3, and physical education) and an English reading class designed specifically for students who do not speak English. My school does not have a specific ESL teacher; the Spanish teachers and a part-time tutor do most of the tutoring for the ESL students. Jorge was so overwhelmed by his schedule that he did what he could to get by and then tended to forget any English he had learned during the previous weeks, unless it was something he used every day.

Jorge was not involved in an official bilingual program; teachers who did not know any Spanish taught him in English for five hours every day. The program we tried to use with Jorge and other students was one class period of immersion in English. We would read, write, and recite English from a book that used phonetic as well as correct spellings to help with pronunciation. The book also included repetitive writing of words and sentences, such as writing each word or sentence three times each. We used this book because there were numerous copies available, bought by the principal for the ESL "lab" at the request of another teacher. For Jorge, and perhaps some of the other students, the books didn't work. He was so focused on doing what the book said—writing the words numerous times—that he would complete three or four chapters in one night for homework without really learning the words. When we insisted he go over the words with us (me, the ESL tutor, and another Spanish teacher), he would refuse, saying he already knew the words. When it came time for quizzes, he would learn the words long enough to do well on the quiz, but on a cumulative test at the end of the year he could not recall most of the words from the beginning of the year. Jorge was frustrated at not knowing the language and being forced to attend classes in which most of his teachers couldn't help him; he, however, isn't completely blameless. He could have put in more effort to aid his learning.

A Teacher Responds

This teacher's story is interesting to me for a number of reasons: first, she seems to have keen insight into the challenges faced by ESL students in schools without real ESL programs, and second, she turns a critical eye toward classroom materials (i.e., workbooks) that may appear to facilitate second language learning but that merely provide opportunities for decontextualized busywork.

This teacher is an English and Spanish teacher in a high school, and therefore she seems to have been given partial duty as an ESL teacher or tutor to students like Jorge. While this is a positive step for many reasons (e.g., it is a good thing that there are adults in the school who speak Jorge's native language and who can communicate with him), it also has some problems. Spanish teachers in the United States are primarily teachers of Spanish as a second language to English-speaking American students. Therefore, they are educated in the cognitive and pedagogical processes of teaching a foreign language to speakers of English who currently reside within an English-speaking culture. Although their ability to communicate in Spanish and their teaching skills may be exemplary, the fact remains that an ESL teacher would be educated in procedures and practices specific to teaching second language learners who are learning English within an English-speaking culture.

The teacher-author of this story seems to recognize the lack of such a teacher in her high school, but she cannot make changes in this system (at least not immediately), and she and the other Spanish teacher and tutor still need to help Jorge succeed. They have workbooks, books that the teacher implies she does not really like; however, they were purchased by another teacher and hence are there to be used. Jorge seems to be working pretty hard; he dutifully does the workbook pages each night, but they do not seem to teach him much, and then he gets frustrated. He is upset because he feels he puts in the work required but doesn't get the promised benefits.

So how could this teacher and her co-teachers have helped Jorge learn English more successfully? They implement some effective strategies with Jorge: they ask him to discuss the words with them, for example, but he is resistant. If possible, I think these teachers should consider foregoing the workbooks the next time they teach the class and opt to use modified assignments from their other English or Spanish classes. In other words, ask the students to read, write, and talk during class. Actually engaging in language activities that have a meaningful context and a real audience has much greater potential for success than the workbook exercises.

The program described here is an example of a pull-out ESL program, which is generally considered one of the weakest approaches to ESL instruction. This teacher, however, clearly knows and cares about her students and wants them to succeed. I suggest she call on the pedagogical knowledge she uses when planning lessons and assignments in her "regular" classes and put this knowledge to use in her ESL class as well. Instead of disregarding the reading, writing, and speaking activities she uses with English-speaking students, I urge her to implement them, with modifications, in the ESL class. She could, for example, incorporate process writing with student texts that begin as oral retellings or are drafted in a home language.

A Teacher Responds

In the story of Jorge, we have a good example of a student who wants to learn and a teacher who has a desire to help the student learn. This is a dynamic combination; in reality, however, it is apparent that not much learning is taking place.

The situation described in this scenario is not unique. In the United States, ESL student populations, once thought to be an issue primarily in urban schools with large populations of linguistically diverse learners, are increasingly popping up in more rural and suburban schools that are both unfamiliar with and underprepared to address the needs of English language learners.

The school highlighted here makes some common but erroneous assumptions about the instruction of culturally and linguistically diverse learners. The first is the assumption that a teacher trained to teach a foreign language in a school in the United States is equipped to teach English to a "foreign" student. In foreign language classes, the type of language taught is social, communicative. As a secondary student, however, what Jorge needs is the academic language that will provide him access to the mainstream curriculum.

Jorge is dedicated but all of his work leads to frustration because he is not developing the English language skills he needs to succeed in his classes. The language development program is, by design, and later by Jorge's choice, heavily based on the workbooks—a form of the old "drill and kill" method. To strengthen the program, there needs to be more balance between the four modalities of language: listening, speaking, reading, and writing. The Spanish teacher realizes that the workbooks are not successful, but her training as a foreign language teacher does not provide her with the skills needed to guide Jorge's academic language and literacy skill development. If use of the workbooks is required, as it seems, then the teacher can expand the workbook exercises to include conversing about the exercises, reading the exercise sentences, pointing to answers as statements are read, and so forth, to expand Jorge's familiarity with not only reading and writing in drill format but also listening and speaking, as well as variations on the drills and exercises. The writing exercises, coupled with listening, speaking, and reading activities done as introductory activities to the written exercises in the workbook, would make for a more expanded and active use of the vocabulary and language that appears in the workbook. It is apparent, however, that the workbooks focus on isolated, rather than integrated, language tasks and do not provide Jorge with the academic language he needs.

The responsibility of teaching Jorge the academic language he needs and providing him access to his curriculum is not the sole responsibility of the Spanish teacher and tutor. Each of Jorge's teachers must take the necessary steps to assist him in developing the language and concepts needed in the individual content areas, as well as provide him with the strategies he needs to navigate the curriculum and work toward achieving challenging academic standards. There are two successful models that integrate the instruction of language and content and therefore can be recommended. The first is the SIOP model (Echevarria, Vogt, & Short, 2000) and the other is CALLA—the cognitive academic language learning approach (Chamot & O'Malley, 1994). Both models have been successfully used by many schools across the United States to teach both language and content while also teaching learning strategies. The Spanish teacher and tutor will not be able to make the language "stick" in the limited amount of time they have with Jorge and without the support of all of Jorge's teachers. Without a team approach such as SIOP or CALLA, Jorge will not get the academic foundation and development he needs to succeed in the mainstream. Content-based instruction is important at all academic levels, but as students enter secondary school, and the amount of time they have to catch up to their native-English-speaking peers decreases, it becomes more important that all teachers employ methods to deliver content-specific modified instruction to accelerate the learning of English language learners in both language and content.

For Further Discussion

1. Thinking back to your high school experience, what was the role of textbooks and workbooks in the English classroom? When and how were they appropriate and helpful? When could they be avoided?

2. How can a teacher help students retain information (such as new words)? In the English classroom, what kinds of activities might be the most helpful when the goal is the retention of language skills and knowledge over time?

3. Think about the importance of teachers teaming or collaborating within and across disciplinary and educational areas. What

are some of the possible benefits of such teaming for both ESL and English-speaking students? What do you think are some of the pros and cons of teaming from a teacher's and from a student's perspective?

Learning Activities

1. With a partner, write a letter to your administrator (or to a hypothetical administrator) requesting the addition of an ESL teacher to your school or department. What reasons would you give for needing such a teacher? What special knowledge might an ESL teacher bring to the school that would improve the educational climate?

2. Conduct some research about the high schools and middle schools in your community. How many of them have ESL programs and ESL teachers? If they have programs, what kind of programs are they? How do they assist and instruct second language learners?

ESL Narrative 3

An important concern in the teaching of ESL students is the issue of identity. Students who are second language speakers have cultural histories that are vital to their self-understanding, self-esteem, and unique identities. If second language teachers ignore these cultural differences or try to erase them from their students' lives in order to create a "classroom as melting pot" situation, ESL students may feel alienated, angry, and confused, feelings that do not foster a rich educational environment. The following story is from a middle school ESL teacher in a suburban public school not far from New York City who finds a way to allow her ESL students to explore the issue of cultural identity while responding to a literary text.

ESL Students and the Loss of Cultural Identity

After I worked with Jim in his eighth-grade classroom as a co-teacher, he shared with me a book he had always taught to his sixth graders. *Julie of the Wolves* by Jean Craighead George was enjoyed by his students, who were in awe of Julie's adventures on the tundra. This book fascinated me too because of Julie's identity dilemma—was she a "gussak" (white American) named Julie or an Eskimo named Miyax? It made me think about many of my ESL students who, once they had somewhat mastered the English language, found themselves losing their native language and cultural identity. Jim had always had his students write a "Who am I?" essay about Julie and her dilemma. But that's as far as he went with the theme, and he was sometimes disappointed with the superficial quality of the students' writing.

I mentioned to Jim that I felt this "Who am I?" was also an issue for my ESL students and that they too would benefit from reading the book in a modified instructional format. But I didn't stop there. I explained that if his students and my students went further into research and projects based on the *Julie* book and the Julie character, maybe they would have a deeper understanding of the conflicts in her life. I proposed that my ESL sixth graders stay in their grade 6 ESL/English class for reading and that we collaborate to work on both miniprojects and one long-term project.

Together we revisited some of the short essay-writing assignments that Jim had done with his students and turned them into paired writing activities for ESL and mainstream partners. We added graphic organizers and taught process writing to help our students. The students mapped Julie's travels throughout the story and wrote descriptive narratives; they wrote about the body language of the wolves, what it meant in "people" language, and what body language their own families used; they wrote about Julie's decisions and debated whether the decisions were her own or if they were made for her; and they compared incidents in their own lives when decisions were made for them and how they had felt. This was particularly poignant for my ESL students, who had often felt confused about having to leave their native countries to come to the United States. The American students connected with their ESL partners because they also felt that moving from one place to another had confused them in the past.

We also read some children's books written by Alaskan authors about children and life in Alaska, Alaskan animals, Inuit folktales, and a book about the Iditarod. We looked at books written in Inuit and other native Eskimo languages. We also looked at books about native crafts, such as totem poles, octopus bags, sun visors, warrior tools, scrimshaw, and soapstone sculpture. This study gave our students a reference point that was real to them about Julie and the people and culture of this very different land.

For long-term projects, we developed four theme choices: challenges of the land (geology, geography, and weather of Alaska); challenges from the animals (animals and insects native to Alaska); challenges for the various cultures and peoples (native Americans, Eskimos, immigrant populations, language, culture); and challenges from history (ownership, discovery of gold, and so forth). Students worked in mixed (ESL and mainstream) groups of four and researched information using books, videos, the Internet, and the Great Alaska Mystery Box (a traveling trunk of information from the Alaska Public Lands Office in Anchorage). They worked together two to three days a week and spent the other days reading *Julie* with their own teachers. All the groups presented their projects for one another and for their second-grade "buddy" who was also studying the Iditarod. The students asked for an "Alaska" night and presented their projects to their parents and families. Their projects were incredibly creative, including plays, games, puppet shows, PowerPoint presentations, and demonstrations.

Finally, the students wrote their *Julie* essay: "Who Am I: Gussak or Eskimo?" We were thrilled with the results. The students wrote with greater depth of understanding of Julie's dilemma and connected it to their own lives. The collaborative efforts of two teachers and many weeks of work were well worth the results.

A Teacher Responds

This story mentions many wonderful strategies and activities that can be beneficial for ESL students. The author talks, for example, about collaboration between ESL and native-English-speaking students; the team-teaching of a mainstream and an ESL teacher; students working on a thematic project that incorporates fiction, nonfiction, and media texts and allows for various modes of student response; and teachers building on ESL students' interests and concerns when developing lessons and assignments.

This teacher tells a success story of a project revolving around *Julie of the Wolves* in middle school English and ESL classrooms. It seems that the collaboration between these two teachers is vital to the reported success. Without the positive working relationship they formed, the author of the narrative might have had no knowledge of Jim's use of the novel and would not have felt as comfortable proposing the collaboration she describes. Clearly, both teachers have strengths that when brought together created a powerful learning experience for both the English-speaking and the ESL students. Jim, the English teacher, chose the novel and devised an essay-writing assignment; the author, an ESL teacher, suggested and implemented modifications to the assignments that involved the addition of thematic, interdisciplinary projects and presentations as well as paired writing assignments and the use of graphic organizers.

Interestingly, the modifications seem to have been as helpful and interesting to the English-speaking students as to the ESL students. I think a common misconception among regular classroom teachers is that if they modify their lessons (e.g., by using a sheltered approach or by spending more time teaching the writing process) they will be "dumbing down" the curriculum and shortchanging the English-speaking students in their classes. This story shows just the opposite: the modifications are examples of exemplary pedagogical practice for *all* students, and they made the *Julie* project even more challenging and satisfying for everyone in the class.

A Teacher Responds

What a great example of working with English language learners! This is an example of education at its finest. Even though they come from different disciplines, these two teachers have developed a successful collaborative model that benefits not only them but also, and more important, all of their students. Both bring their strengths and backgrounds to the team while respecting and accepting the other. This provides a strong collaborative team model. Their roles as collaborators also provide an excellent model for their students to emulate, and the fact that they are comfortable with each other creates an educationally rich environment.

Because they come from two different arenas in education, these teachers look at the book, *Julie of the Wolves,* from different perspectives. Jim, in his role as language arts teacher, sees the book as a piece of literature, which can be read and discussed and which provides a springboard for a writing assignment. The ESL teacher sees a story with a theme to which she knows her English language learners can relate.

Another positive to the arrangement presented is that the ESL students get to stay in the grade 6 class and work with the native speakers. For middle school students, the positive impact of this move is far beyond the obvious. Middle schoolers are constantly reassessing themselves and their relationships, acceptances, and rejections. Having all students work together on a common project to which the ESL students are active contributors has tremendous potential to increase the self-esteem of these students, who often feel that they are on the fringes of their school societies. In addition, the students acquiring the English language have the opportunity to work one-on-one with a native-English-speaking peer who provides a functioning model for the English language.

Often when we see English language learners working together with native English speakers, we see them as observers, with little to bring to the group because of their limited language skills or cultural experiences. In this case, however, the ESL students can play a major role in the discussion *because* they come from another culture. They were able to share some of their own experiences as adolescents struggling between two cultures and increase the comprehension of Julie's identity dilemma for all of the students. This is another plus in the self-esteem column.

I find it interesting that the book selected, which discusses cultural conflicts and dilemmas, is actually a book about an American. This in itself is a powerful statement for native speakers who may experience cultural prejudice daily in a variety of ways. Additionally, the ESL students see an American child dealing with many of the same issues with which they are dealing.

The use of "realia," or classroom activities that relate to real-life situations, is also interesting. Often a tool used in ESL classes, realia here gave students in one geographic section of the United States a clearer understanding of the lives of others in a different part of this country. Realia allowed the teachers to shed light on the Alaskan culture, not only for the ESL students but for the traditional students as well.

This scenario illustrates an excellent example of what can be accomplished when teachers work collaboratively in lesson planning to develop powerful lessons for all students.

For Further Discussion

1. Why do you think thematic units of instruction might work especially well for ESL students?

2. *Julie of the Wolves* is an example of a young adult novel. Recalling what you read about YA books in Chapter 1, why does a YA book have a good chance of working well with ESL students? Are there any strategies discussed in Chapter 1 as best practices in literature instruction that could also be effective with ESL students? Why or why not?

3. Think back to the challenges of being an adolescent entering a new school or entering middle school or high school. What do you remember about issues or problems with fitting in? Now think of entering the same school from the point of view of a new immigrant.

Learning Activities

1. In a small group, find and list examples of YA books that address themes and issues that might be of particular interest to second language learners.

2. After reading the narrative "ESL Students and the Loss of Cultural Identity," write an assignment sheet for the *Julie* essay the author describes that could be given to students. Include a context and audience for the writing, the concrete parameters of the paper (length, formatting, due date of drafts, etc.), and a description of the issue or topic the paper should address. Allow as much room as possible for individual student variation and choice.

ESL Narrative 4

The teacher in the following narrative is perceptive about the nature of the language learning taking place among her students. She realizes that dictionaries, both English-only and dual language, can be useful tools for ESL (or ELL) students. She also recognizes, however, the difficulties such dictionaries can cause when students do not completely understand the nuances of dictionary use and how dictionaries are compiled. In this story, an English/ESL teacher in a suburban, midwestern high school with about 1,700 students in grades 9 through 12 tells of a student named Ankhar who uses a dual-language dictionary to complete an assignment. He discovers that dictionaries have cultural differences that can create significant misunderstandings. Ankhar's teacher is certified in both English and ESL instruction, and Ankhar's English language arts class is geared specifically for second language learners.

Dictionary Use and Language Learning

Dictionary usage is an important skill to be developed with all students; however, instructing students whose first language is not English about how to use a dictionary must go beyond the obvious.

All of the secondary English language learners (ELLs) were reading a story about a boy who had lost his backpack in school. The two-page story was written using basic grammatical sentence structures and vocabulary and explained all the things the boy had in his backpack: textbooks, notebooks, a pen, a pencil, a ruler, an eraser, a candy bar, photographs, etc. All the listed items appeared in a word bank with pictures, making the vocabulary more comprehensible. At

▶

the end of the selection were ten simple questions. The answers being elicited were all from the lower level of Bloom's taxonomy. The selection was appropriate in every way for a group of high-beginning and low-intermediate ELLs.

Most of the students in class carried dictionaries with them. While they were encouraged to use English-only dictionaries, many times they were stumped and resorted to their dual-language dictionaries for explanations or confirmation of a word meaning.

Ankhar had finished reading the selection and begun working on the questions at the end. His English skills were weaker than the others in the class, but he had managed to complete the reading without using a dictionary. He completed questions one through nine with little difficulty, but he seemed to be spending a lot of time on question ten. "What happened to the boy at the end of the story?" was the question giving Ankhar so much trouble. He picked up his dual-language dictionary, went back to the final paragraph of the story, and looked up a word. He double checked the word and the definition and then crossed out the answers from questions one through nine. Next to number ten he wrote, "The boy got drunk."

The last sentence of the reading selection was: "When the bell rang at the end of the day, the boy was still looking for his backpack." The word that had given Ankhar trouble was *still*. When Ankhar looked up the word in his dual-language dictionary, the information he found there skewed his entire understanding of the story.

Definitions are listed in dictionaries in the order of frequency with which the words are used in a given language. In an English dictionary, the definitions are ordered according to the frequency of the definition in the English language; in a Spanish dictionary, the words are ordered according to their frequency in the Spanish language; in a Korean dictionary, the definitions are ordered according to their frequency in the Korean language, and so on. Because word usage and frequency vary from language to language, definition number one in the English dictionary does not necessarily equate to definition number one of that word in a dictionary in another language.

When Ankhar looked up the word *still* in his native-language dictionary, the first definition stated that a still was a place where alcohol was made. This gave him the misconception that the story had something to do with the boy drinking, which affected his entire perception of the story. Just one word caused him to go back and cross out all of his correct answers.

Dictionaries are extremely useful tools in a classroom, and for English language learners, they are a must. As with all secondary students, however, when they look up words they rarely go beyond the first, or possibly second, definition. Proper use of a dual-language dictionary is an important skill, and students must be specifically instructed in that proper usage. It is equally important for teachers to check on the definitions students select, particularly students at the lower levels of English language development.

A Teacher Responds

This teacher discusses a language skill that many of us take for granted and believe that all students can figure out pretty much on their own: using the dictionary. But as this story shows, all dictionaries are not created equal. Dictionaries have cultural differences, just as students do, and these differences are based on language variations that are more complex than simply the translation of one word into another. The teacher discovers that when students resort to dual-language dictionaries, the order of the definitions of a word translated into another language can be different; hence, students may choose the wrong definition for an English word and misunderstand a text. Her point is well taken—teachers of ESL students should explain how a dictionary is compiled, what the order of the definitions means, and how this order might vary depending on the culture and language the dictionary represents. One idea this story suggests is that the students, whether English-speaking or ESL, in a class where such explanation is given might learn that authors and editors create texts (including dictionaries) and make systematic choices about how the texts will be assembled. Thus, students can begin to see texts as purposeful, and sometimes political, artifacts that they can learn to understand, rather than untouchable creations that seem to have fallen from the sky intact. In the English classroom, we tend to treat texts this way: as valuable, priceless objects that were created by a genius. While this description might be true in some cases, it is not true that the text is above critique or critical understanding. Although a dictionary might not be the most powerful example of a text to ask students to deconstruct, it strikes me as one of the most ubiquitous and hence one most ripe for deconstruction. Why are certain words included and not others? Why are certain definitions placed before others? These are thoughtful questions students could ask and respond to as they become more sophisticated language users.

Another interesting point about this story is that Ankhar's understanding of the definition of *still* changes his understanding of the *entire* passage, and he goes back to his earlier answers and changes them to correspond with the new definition. This is a powerful example of how context can affect comprehension. After having read the definition of *still* as a mechanism for making alcohol, Ankhar had to rethink the entire text to fit it into this alcohol-related context. Of course, his conclusions were incorrect, but his thinking processes and language skills were right on target. Ankhar's story reminds the teacher of ESL students (and of English-speaking students) of the importance of context in reading comprehension and how taking time to create an understandable (and relevant) context for textual meaning can make a significant difference in the quality of student understanding and response.

A Teacher Responds

Students often have a strong dependence on bilingual dictionaries, and errors such as this one often occur due to this dependence. Part of the problem, I think, is that ELLs are "word" readers rather than phrase, clause, or sentence readers. They spend a large amount of time reading one word at a time and not using the context for meaning clues. Possibly this student would have more accurately determined the meaning at the end of the passage if he had used the other words and phrases—*backpack, end of the day, bell rang*—as clues to the choice of definition for *still.* But this technique doesn't come naturally to second language learners. Although they may use the context to determine meaning in their native language, they do not know how to transfer that technique to a second language. This skill must be taught.

One of the "using the context" techniques I've modeled with students is to overview the passage before reading. We look through the passage for the words *or* and *like.* We then highlight these words in one color, say yellow or light green. We then go back and highlight the words around *or* or *like* with the other color highlighter. Then we read the entire phrases containing both highlighted colors and hypothesize about the meanings. *Or* will give us a synonym for the word and *like* will give us examples of how the word is used (e.g., exoskeleton, like lobsters or crabs). To check our hypotheses, we then use the dictionary to look at the choices of meanings for the word. Without the dictionary, we can also practice a think-aloud strategy: "Lobsters and crabs have claws and crawl and they also have shells, not bones on the inside like people and other animals. So maybe *exoskeleton* means 'outside shell.' I remember the science teacher also told us that some animals have their bones on the outside, not like us. We have our bones on the inside. So maybe *exoskeleton* means 'skeleton on the outside.'"

After a lot of practice, students can often determine meaning without using the dictionary for every word. This is only one technique that has worked with my middle school students. In fact, they often tell me with pride in their discovery, "Look, there's an *or* here. The word means . . ."

For Further Discussion

1. What might be the benefits of students "deconstructing" or analyzing the dictionary as a text?

2. In your experience in middle or high school, how did English teachers use dictionaries in their classes? Did you find such use effective? Why or why not?

3. The teacher in the second response gives an example of how to help students pay attention to context when figuring out new words. Can you think of additional ways students can be taught to be more effective readers? In a group, list some strategies that good readers use to make meaning from texts, beginning with context clues.

Learning Activities

1. In a collaborative group, create an assignment that asks students to look critically at an English or dual-language dictionary. What might you ask students to do? What questions might you provide to guide their analysis?

2. Discuss with your peers or colleagues what Ankhar's story might demonstrate or reveal about teaching reading to both ESL and English-speaking students.

In Closing

This chapter provides an overview of the challenges of and possibilities for teaching the ESL student in the secondary English classroom. We realize that this topic is not addressed often enough in English-teaching pedagogy courses, and we hope this oversight is diminishing. ESL students are becoming more prevalent in secondary schools nationwide, and English teachers must be prepared to instruct such students effectively. Often the instructional modifications made in classes containing ESL students can also be positive changes for English-speaking students, as we think the narratives in the chapter demonstrate.

Too many Americans are resistant to the increasing visibility of people representing other cultures (and hence speaking other languages) in the United States, and sadly, this resistance can lead to oppressive laws and even violence directed toward various ethnic and minority groups that are viewed as the "other." The pedagogical strategies outlined in this chapter can facilitate the learning of ESL and English-speaking students, but perhaps more important, these practices can lead to increased collaboration among U.S. and immigrant teenagers, and such collaboration might result in cross-cultural friendships, mutual understanding, and respect.

We hope this chapter will help you as you continue to think about and develop your own philosophy of teaching second language learners in the secondary English classroom. As a concluding activity, write a short statement describing your philosophy of teaching ESL students in the English class. Try to begin to answer some of the following questions as you describe your current or future classroom practices when teaching second language learners and the beliefs that guide them:

1. What are my goals for the ESL students in my classroom?
2. How might my teaching change/not change because of ESL learners?
3. What other school personnel might I call on to assist in my instruction of ESL students?
4. What can I do to increase my level of preparation for teaching ESL students?
5. How can ESL students enrich my classroom?

Additional Texts about the Teaching of ESL Students in the English Classroom

Books

Agor, Barbara (Ed.). (2000). *Integrating the ESL Standards into Classroom Practice: Grades 9–12.* Alexandria, VA: Teachers of English to Speakers of Other Languages.

This book is divided into chapters that describe instructional units for high school ESL classrooms that successfully integrate ESL standards while teaching content.

Irujo, Suzanne (Ed.). (2000). *Integrating the ESL Standards into Classroom Practice: Grades 6–8.* Alexandria, VA: Teachers of English to Speakers of Other Languages.

> This book is divided into chapters that describe instructional units for middle school ESL classrooms that successfully integrate ESL standards while teaching content.

Short, Deborah J. (Ed.). (1999). *New Ways in Teaching English at the Secondary Level.* Alexandria, VA: Teachers of English to Speakers of Other Languages.

> This book is a collection of best practices in teaching ESL students in secondary schools. The lessons described were created by real teachers and could be replicated and implemented easily by English and ESL teachers. Topics include making connections with content areas, multimedia instruction, collaborative projects, and icebreakers to start the school year.

Silva, Tony, and Paul Kei Matsuda (Eds.). (2001). *Landmark Essays on ESL Writing.* Mahwah, NJ: Erlbaum.

> This is a collection of essays that the editors designate as important or foundational in the study of the ESL writer, predominantly at the postsecondary level.

Teachers of English to Speakers of Other Languages. (1997). *ESL Standards for Pre-K–12 Students.* Alexandria, VA: Author.

> This book contains the goals and standards for pre-K–12 ESL education as developed and disseminated by TESOL. It also includes a discussion of the rationale for creating the standards and vignettes describing how the standards might be implemented in real classrooms.

Electronic Resources

National Clearinghouse for English Language Acquisition (NCELA)
www.ncela.gwu.edu/

> This page is sponsored by NCELA, an organization funded by the U.S. Department of Education's Office of English Language Acquisition, Language Enhancement, and Academic Achievement for Limited English Proficient Students. The role of NCELA is to disseminate information about the effective education of linguistically and culturally diverse students in the United States. This site provides links to many resources, including articles, informa-

tion about laws relating to ESL instruction, upcoming conferences that might be of interest, and pedagogical stories.

Teaching English to Speakers of Other Languages (TESOL)
www.tesol.org/

This page provides information about the TESOL organization as well as many resources for second language teachers at various levels. There is also a link to the TESOL standards for pre-K–12 instruction.

5 Narratives about Three Professional Issues: Management and Discipline, Technology, and Testing

When we solicited real-life stories for this book, we anticipated some topics we wanted to discuss but did not have a sense of the types of stories we would receive. We ended up developing chapters around those issues that are commonly understood as central to the teaching of English language arts (writing, literature, grammar) and also those that were unplanned but for which we received interesting narratives from teachers (English as a second language). This left us with some strong stories we wanted to include but without a chapter to put them in. Therefore, this chapter centers on narratives that describe important aspects of teaching English language arts that aren't always discussed explicitly and completely in preservice education: classroom management, technology, and standardized testing. We include shorter versions of the informational categories present in earlier chapters: discussions of current conceptions of best practices, a narrative, a response, questions for discussion, and additional, useful resources.

A Discussion of Classroom Management and Discipline

This first issue is one that we often hear from past students in the "why didn't we talk about this more?" category. The importance of classroom management is often overstated to the detriment of curriculum, but the simple fact remains that a teacher who does not develop a culture of learning and respect is often doomed never to see his or her classroom goals fulfilled. We have seen too many promising young teachers disillusioned and disoriented with their teaching experiences because of their inability to effectively manage their classrooms. Classroom management and discipline are by far the most common difficulties and stressors noted by the student teachers with whom we work. We did not want to make classroom management a focus of this book since we believe that effective classroom management is a by-product of effective pedagogy. We recognize, however, that disciplinary and management problems are a reality in secondary education, and teacher educators are remiss to ignore them.

Classroom management in English language arts can be a complex endeavor. Most English teachers work to develop their classrooms as active learning environments, with small groups, discussions, hands-on activities, and other student-centered methods. These methods can create strong curricula but, paradoxically, often add to the burden of classroom management. How can teachers maintain standards of discipline and management while also realizing the potential of an exciting reading and writing environment? Each teacher must develop his or her classroom management practices based on careful consideration of known systems and theories, coupled with an awareness of personal style, curricular goals, and the particular teaching-learning context. Additionally, a teacher's self-concept, level of self-esteem, and expectations of others influence how successful he or she is in managing a class.

Experienced English language arts teacher Leila Christenbury (2000) offers the following advice:

> Discipline seems a simple concept, but it is actually very complex and is the sum of a number of variables, not the least of which is the beginning teacher's rather nascent perception of what is acceptable behavior and what is not. . . . [W]hat you assume to be polite or respectful behavior between teachers and students may not, indeed, be what your students assume. The only way to determine this is to watch and learn, ask and adjust your own expectations—and, yes, you have the right to have those expectations—to the reality of your school context. (p. 53–54)

The following general tips on how to effectively manage classrooms and begin to create rich learning environments are suggested by Discipline by Design's *Honor Level System* (www.honorlevel.com) (Churchward, 2003). It is important to note that these techniques, like all management concepts, are not a panacea for classroom management or disciplinary issues. Instead, they should be looked at as possible ideas for creating individual management and disciplinary plans.

- *Focusing:* techniques that gain student attention before a lesson begins—standard activities to start a class, rituals, routines
- *Direct Instruction:* telling students exactly what is going to occur; this is meant to alleviate uncertainty and immediately sets limits and goals
- *Monitoring:* staying in contact with students and groups; circulating through the class and being aware of all activities in the class

- *Modeling:* the attitude and behavior of the teacher will be reflected in the students
- *Nonverbal Cuing:* nonverbal cues can often become stereotyped as the "lights out" and other techniques, but signals that direct without talking can be effective
- *Environmental Control:* the classroom environment should be developed in ways that support the desired tone and fit the teacher's lessons and goals
- *Low-Profile Intervention:* trying to defuse confrontations keeps students from escalating a confrontation; keep interventions firm, but polite
- *Assertive Discipline:* setting boundaries and consequences; clear rules and expectations
- *Positive Discipline:* using classroom rules that describe what a student should be doing instead of what he or she is doing wrong

Narrative 1: Classroom Management

Set in an urban high school classroom in the Southwest, the following narrative describes a new teacher's struggle to move toward an effective classroom management system during his first year of teaching. This is a common experience for many teachers.

The Difficult Class: A First-Year Teacher Struggles to Gain Control

I came into teaching with confidence, a lot of confidence (a bit too much, truthfully). I had been a successful camp counselor over the years and had a good student-teaching experience. After years of leading camp songs, telling stories, and teaching classes such as sailing and canoeing, I *knew* that kids liked me. Hey, I was the cool guy, the one who told all the jokes, who knew all the new movies. Classroom management would be a breeze, right?

The answer, of course, was an emphatic *no!* Teaching ninth-grade English was not the same as teaching sailing. Yeah, kids still liked me; I was still funny, but the honeymoon was wearing thin, quickly. I could feel the control slipping from my grasp.

Around early November of my first year, my difficulties began to come to a head. In particular, I could feel my fifth-hour class becoming restless, the class stocked with the "good" kids—not honor

▶

students exactly, but through the quirky scheduling of band and chorus, an inordinate number of upper-echelon students. What was happening? Too much noise, for one thing. I'm okay with some noise; in fact, I tend to like it. But this was not productive talk, and I was powerless to stop it.

What else? Tone. Humor was becoming disrespectful—to me and to other students. What was once good-natured kidding became jokes about acne, weight, and other teen afflictions. Attention. Whereas before I could expect to get my students' attention when I needed it, I now found myself yelling just to get their attention. The beginning of class was becoming a five-minute ordeal: getting out books, shuffling papers, finishing conversations from breaks.

Nothing really bad had happened yet, but I could feel it coming. I couldn't envision how I could manage this class throughout the entire year. I was getting worn down, and I found myself becoming the type of teacher I always hated. I once heard myself yell, "Shut up!"

It's now winter break. My New Year's resolution: get control of my classes. The other classes hadn't "advanced" as quickly as this one, but I could see it coming.

A Teacher Responds

As much as I hate to admit it, this teacher's first year sounds a lot like mine, and I'm sure I'm not alone. Classroom management is consistently the most difficult adjustment most new teachers face. They are usually relatively close in age to their students, and they are worried about students liking them. Also, new teachers often find themselves under pressure from colleagues and administrators to "control" their classes more firmly, although they don't always receive very specific advice about how to do so. The result can be frustration and feelings of failure. My first inclination, then, is to sympathize and offer my support. But I can also offer some advice:

I have so many things to ask: Is he planning effectively? Is there too much time left over at the end of class, providing space for misbehavior to occur? Has he thought about how he structures the classroom to minimize chatter? Are students given guidelines, for example, for group assignments? Are they held accountable through grades or other types of evaluation for seat and group work?

First, much like any other problem, the first step to successfully combating it is to admit that there *is* a problem. I must applaud the teacher for this. Too many new teachers are embarrassed by their class-room management problems. As a result, they tend to close their doors and hope their veteran colleagues won't notice.

I would encourage this teacher to find someone he trusts to talk to in his own building. There are reasons why veteran colleagues are still there. They have developed techniques that work in their own class-rooms. They may not all be people to whom you feel comfortable talk-ing, but by communicating with other teachers, you can get a sense of different successful techniques that might be used and develop a rep-ertoire of ways to get control of your classroom.

More specifically for this classroom, the teacher needs to find a way to nurture a sense of respect in students for their teacher and their peers. Students are being disrespectful not only to him but also to one another. And they know exactly what they are doing—pushing the en-velope on behavior. There are many disciplinary and management sys-tems available for secondary teachers (e.g., Assertive Discipline and Love and Logic), and I would recommend looking at them but not adapting them in their entirety. Instead, he should go through and pick and choose different techniques that seem to fit his classroom ideals.

I would also urge the teacher to develop a system that is consis-tent with his personality. He seems to have a lot of enthusiasm, and I am sure that his class is both interesting and fun for students. I would hate to see that excitement and innovation taken out of the classroom for a check-mark system. Ultimately, he needs to find a happy medium between his natural tendency to want to run a "fun" classroom and his need to create a means by which mutual respect becomes natural. Some things he might want to explore include:

- an opening activity (journal writing, vocabulary, daily-oral lan-guage, or others) that students know they will be immediately accountable for. This will create a more serious and academic environment that he will not have to continually manage;
- a class-developed set of rules and standards. He should set up some basic premises and have students develop some others. He could set it up as a collaborative writing assignment that the class does immediately on returning from vacation. Included in these rules should be consequences and means of account-ability.

For Further Discussion

1. What are some of the best and the worst examples of class-room management or discipline you have witnessed either as a student or as a teacher? What did you learn from these ex-amples?

2. From your experiences and observations, what techniques could you suggest this new teacher employ to get immediate improvement in the management of his classroom?

Learning Activities

1. Type in the phrases "classroom management" or "classroom discipline" in a World Wide Web search engine. What is the range of results you receive? What systems and/or concepts seem applicable to your situation?

2. In a small group, create a list of rules or guidelines that this teacher could post in his room.

Additional Resources about Classroom Management and Discipline

There are many books and professional development seminars about classroom management available. Some of these include:

Canter, Lee, and Marlene Canter. (1997). *Lee Canter's Assertive Discipline Audiocassette Program: Positive Behavior Management for Today's Classroom* [Sound recording]. Santa Monica, CA: Canter and Associates.

This is perhaps the best known of the many systems available. It's designed to help teachers cultivate a productive learning environment in the classroom. These tapes support the written text.

Canter, Lee, and Marlene Canter. (2002). *Assertive Discipline: Positive Behavior Management for Today's Classroom.* Santa Monica, CA: Canter and Associates.

This book, in its third edition, describes a behavior management plan that is consistent with effective teaching techniques. *Assertive Discipline* attempts to take a proactive approach to dealing with discipline.

Curwin, Richard L., and Allen N. Mendler. (1994). *Curwin & Mendler's Discipline with Dignity* [Videorecording]. Bloomington, IL: National Education Service.

This approach discusses three steps—prevention, action, and resolution—that can be taken to obtain discipline in the classroom while preserving the dignity of both students and teacher.

Education World's Teacher Resources: Classroom Management
http://db.education-world.com

Like Teachnet.com, this site collects a variety of resources on the topic of classroom management, including tips for organizing space, connecting with parents, and creating assignments.

Fay, Jim, and David Funk. (1998). *Teaching with Love and Logic: Taking Control of the Classroom* [Sound recording]. Golden, CO: Love and Logic Press.

The plans of Fay and Funk describe how discipline can be administered in ways that do not humiliate students or frustrate the teacher and that result in changes to students' beliefs about preferred behavior. Most of these texts have value if taken in context and viewed with a critical eye.

Teacher Talk: What Is Your Classroom Management Profile?
http://education.Indiana.edu/cas/tt/v1i2/what.html

This Web site is an essential resource for practicing and preservice teachers who want to critically consider their classroom management techniques and concepts. This site asks a series of questions and then points participants to four different profiles of classroom management (authoritarian, authoritative, laissez-faire, and indifferent).

Teachnet.com's "Classroom Management" Topic Index
www.teachnet.com/how-to/manage/

This is a useful site that does not espouse a specific stance on classroom management but instead consolidates various resources for teachers seeking ideas.

A Discussion of Teaching with Technology

That technology has affected the ways we teach English language arts is undeniable. English teachers are envisioning literacy in ways unimaginable just a few years ago. Technology is often lauded as being revolutionary, with the promise of improving student engagement through its mere presence in the classroom. But there are also issues and difficulties in integrating technologies into the English language arts classroom. We are committed to teaching with technologies and taking advantage of the new possibilities it provides, but we are also committed to helping English language arts teachers make the best use of those technologies. In other words, it is important to know how to use certain hardware and software, but it is equally important for teachers to know how such technology can be used to teach their content more effectively.

Let's consider the pervasive technology offered by Microsoft PowerPoint, a presentation software that has become standard in teaching and business contexts from elementary school to executive board meetings. The most immediate benefits of this program are easy to identify: Students can easily create presentations for class that use snappy visual and audio cues. Students will become more engaged, they will see that writing can be used for more than just essays, and they can see a tangible need for quality since they will most likely be presenting this work in front of their peers or another audience. The decision to use PowerPoint, then, should be an easy one. When we look more closely at the program, however, we can also see some problems. PowerPoint has a tendency to dictate communication in short bulleted points; move presenters toward simplistic notions; and, with the tendency of inexperienced presenters to overuse flashy visuals, can lead to the implicit message that style is more important than content. Additionally, students (and teachers) can get so caught up in the fun of using PowerPoint that they forget why they chose to use it.

Does this mean that we shouldn't use PowerPoint as a classroom technology? We think it does have a place in the English language arts classroom. We also believe, however, that teachers should consider not only *how* but also *why* they wish to use it with students. Another interesting technological capability that can be integrated into the classroom is online discussion or chat. Many teachers regularly use e-mail to communicate with colleagues, students, and parents. Asking students to participate in listserv discussions or synchronous (real time) chats, however, can provide writing practice and build fluency with language. Many adolescents spend hours every day writing back and forth with friends in chat rooms. But when they come to their English class, they might say they hate to write! Some educators have noticed that students are using chat room abbreviations and modified spellings in essays written for class; while this may not be appropriate or desirable, teachers might capitalize on the popularity of chats and online discussions when teaching writing. Discussing the concepts of genre and audience with students could be a good way to help them understand that the language they use in chats or in online discussions might not be the language of choice for a literary essay and vice versa. Helping students understand that what they are doing online is actually *writing* and *reading* might improve their attitudes toward English class.

Teachers regularly assign research writing to their students, and many students these days do research on the World Wide Web. Sometimes, however, students don't know how to evaluate the quality of Web sites and therefore treat them all as equal authorities on a topic. Again, this is a perfect teachable moment: students can consider the qualities of Web sites that demonstrate that they are trustworthy and valid. They can ask questions such as Who is the author(s) of this site? Why did the author(s)s create this site? Is this site connected with a larger organization, company, or group? If so, what is the nature of this connection? Is the site linked to any other sites? Which ones and why? Can you compare this site to others on the topic? If so, do they contain any similar information, or is this site alone in making certain claims? Such questions can teach students to be critical readers of Internet and media texts and more thorough researchers.

Teachers must consider not only the surface benefits of bringing technology into their classrooms but also the potential limitations and problems. Thus, when we begin to think about using technologies in our class, we should ask questions such as the following:

- Why do I want to use technologies?
- How can the technologies enhance my ability to reach curricular goals and content standards?
- What are my students capable of handling? How much previous experience have they had with technology?
- What am I capable of handling? How comfortable and knowledgeable am I about technology?
- What technologies are available and how can they be used in the English class?
- When I have my students compose with technologies such as PowerPoint or Web designing software such as Dreamweaver or FrontPage, am I teaching them how to apply a process of composing and consider rhetorical goals such as audience and purpose?
- How am I going to assess technology projects? Do I want to evaluate only how well students can use the software or hardware, or do I want to assess the quality of their product as well? If so, what are the characteristics of a high-quality electronic document?
- How can I adapt to a limited access to technologies in my school?

The answers to these questions should begin to guide English teachers' integration of technology into their classes.

Narrative 2: Technology

This narrative takes place in an urban charter school in the Midwest and illustrates a teacher's work with newly integrated technologies. In his school's struggles, we see many of the common problems associated with technology (along with the possibilities): system failures, classroom management, and faculty misunderstanding of how to use technology effectively.

Constructive Chaos: Teaching with Technology

I was surprised. It actually happened the way it was supposed to happen. One morning my first-hour students were working in groups on their writing, sharing excerpts and revising their peers' work in constructive, meaningful ways. They were so deeply engaged that when the bell rang, very few even heard it. I had somehow created a learning community that fostered this degree of engagement.

I teach in a public charter high school that is, according to our governor, "the most diverse school in the state" (in terms of race, ethnicity, socioeconomic class, and life experiences). After having worked through numerous diversity-related issues, my students were writing together, in heterogeneously mixed groups, using school-owned laptop computers.

The teachers and administrators involved in the planning phase of our school technology project made a decision to allocate a sizable portion of our state funds toward the purchase of laptop computers, which, they envisioned, would give students access to primary sources and allow them to create multimedia projects and more easily publish their work. This vision, we soon discovered, was much more difficult to enact than it was to imagine, as issues related to classroom management and our infrastructure appeared. Disk drives erased student work, hard drives crashed, classroom printers routinely jammed, network connections failed during lessons dependent on Internet availability. Likewise, students found it impossible to walk to and from the printer without interfering (in the words of one teacher) with the work of other groups. In short, the technology bred an atmosphere of relative chaos to the point that many teachers, particularly those disposed to more structured classrooms, ultimately decided to take the computers out of their classrooms as well as their curricula.

▷

In this regard, I may be something of an anomaly. I embraced the chaos. A bustling classroom meant that students were engaged and learning was happening. The technology issues were often frustrating, and at times nearly overwhelming. But to terminate the use of the laptops for writing would have ended the smiles I saw on my students' faces as they printed a draft of their work, the intermittent sharing and exchanges that occurred on the walk to and from the printer, and the enthusiasm as they peered over the shoulders of their classmates to see what was on their computer screens. In short, neither my students nor I could have experienced what we did without the computers and the atmosphere of "chaos" they helped create.

For me, the promise of technology seems limited only by a teacher's capacity to relinquish ownership of the classroom to students and to challenge his or her definition of a teacher by imaging the potential of a technology-rich classroom supporting diverse learning styles. I cannot say for certain why my classroom worked that morning, or how it happened. But the image of my students—four heads pressed together as they gazed into their classmate's computer screen—will forever remind me of what is possible with technology.

A Teacher Responds

This teacher is one I would like to have on my faculty. His ability to see past the initial problems and stick with the laptops impresses me, and I am glad to see that he continues to use them.

Yes, bringing technologies into a classroom can be tricky. Even with the best-made plans, things can still be difficult. I personally helped in the development of my own school's computer lab, and I was sure that we had figured out all the bugs. Of course, once the computers were installed, a whole new set of problems appeared.

My main advice to this teacher is to assume a leadership role among his faculty. It is great that he is doing well with the computers. But what about the rest of the staff and their students? The vast amount of money spent on those computers will be wasted if they are not used. He needs to reach out to the teachers who "decided to take the computers out of their classrooms." How could he do this? There are two ways of initiating this leadership role: formally and informally. It is unclear from the narrative how long this teacher has been teaching at his school. If he has several years of experience and a positive collaborative relationship with his colleagues, it will be easier for him to facilitate faculty workshops or request the purchase of educational materials to share with the more reluctant faculty. These types of activities would have to be sanctioned and supported by this teacher's administration. Less formal ways of providing technology mentorship and leadership would involve one-on-one conversations with colleagues about technology issues or problems. This teacher might, for example, drop by a colleague's room during her prep period and ask her how technology is working in her classes—then offer to help if she requests assistance. Both formal and informal interventions have the potential to change how technology is viewed and used in this teacher's school. If students are to become skillful users of technology, they must experience its potential in many content areas, not just in the English class taught by this teacher.

For Further Discussion

1. Based on your experiences and observations in classes, what do you think are the problems and potentials of technology in the English classroom? What examples of technology do you think can be effective additions to the English language arts curriculum? Why and how?

2. Students come from a wide array of backgrounds and therefore have very different experiences with technology. Students from middle- or upper-class families might have grown up with computers and be comfortable using them. Students from less advantaged socioeconomic backgrounds may be much less confident because they did not grow up with computers in their homes. Brainstorm ways to structure technology-based assignments or activities so that you don't assume too much prior knowledge, comfort, or experience.

Learning Activities

1. In a small group, select three to five types of technology that could be used in the English class: e.g., computers, word-processing software, projection equipment, PowerPoint, Web development software, Internet access, chat rooms, etc. Additionally, consider how this technology could be integrated into existing curricula in order to enhance learning.

2. Conduct research to discover ten to fifteen types of educational software that are available for educators to purchase for classroom use. Examples include grammar- and spell-checkers, reference guides, games, software teaching stages of the writing process, "comment" features for word-processing software, etc. How do the makers of this software claim to help adolescent learners with their products? How effective do you think they might be?

Additional Resources about Using Technology in the English Classroom

English Journal, 90(2), November 2000 issue.

> This technology-themed issue contains excellent discussions of why and why not to use technologies in English language arts classrooms.

Greenlaw, Jim, and Jazlin V. Ebenezer (Eds.). (2001). *English Language Arts and Reading on the Internet: A Resource for K–12 Teachers.* Upper Saddle River, NJ: Prentice Hall.

> This is a resource book for teachers that offers many practical ideas for using the Internet to teach reading, writing, speaking, and listening. It also provides a list of language arts Web sites appropriate for and useful in the secondary classroom.

Gruber, Sibylle. (Ed.). (2000). *Weaving a Virtual Web: Practical Approaches to New Information Technologies.* Urbana, IL: National Council of Teachers of English.

> This is a collection of essays written by teachers at different levels and in various contexts about using the World Wide Web in the classroom. Web-based research is addressed as well as pedagogical and theoretical reasons for using the Internet in class.

Moeller, Dave. (2002). *Computers in the Writing Classroom.* Urbana, IL: National Council of Teachers of English.

> This is NCTE's first book to discuss in depth the use of technology in an English language arts context. The author gives a strong overview of the guiding concepts and practices that make for effective integration of technology in classrooms.

Oregon Writing Project at Willamette University's "Manifesto of Writing and Technology"
www.willamette.org/owp/pages/tech/principles.html

> This is an excellent guide for teachers considering combining computers and writing. The site lays out some key principles for writing teachers when considering the effective use of technology in their classrooms.

Western Michigan University's Teaching English through Technology
www.wmich.edu/teachenglish

> This site describes uses of technology in English language arts

classrooms and provides critical discussions of when and how technology can be effectively integrated in these classrooms.

A Discussion of Standardized Testing

Standardized testing is an issue that evokes strong emotions in most English language arts teachers. Standardized tests are tests created by committees of educators, politicians, and citizens (sometimes with the help of an educational publishing company) to be given to large groups of students in a state or region. The scores on such tests (usually primarily multiple-choice tests, although some require writing) are used for various purposes, including certifying students for high school graduation (high-stakes tests), evaluating schools and teachers, and, in the best of worlds, improving classroom teaching.

With good reason, our field often views standardized testing negatively. Generally, we are opposed to the current growth in standardized testing and the belief that increased testing is synonymous with increased learning, and we recognize the potentially harmful effects of high-stakes testing on students, teachers, and schools. The current push for "accountability" that began in the 1970s is in part the result of harsh judgments of teachers and the widespread belief that U.S. public education is in crisis, a belief that began with the publication of *A Nation at Risk* in 1983 (National Commission on Excellence). We are not going to use this space to repeat arguments against standardized testing with which you are probably already familiar, but we encourage readers to critically analyze some of these arguments by visiting Web sites like www.fairtest.org and reading books written by antitesting advocates such as Alfie Kohn (2000) and Susan Ohanian (1999). You might also be interested in researching how and why U.S. schools have been deemed inadequate (see Gerald W. Bracey's *What You Should Know about the War against America's Public Schools* [2003]).

While English teachers and their professional organizations have been vocal in opposing standardized tests, such as those mandated under the No Child Left Behind Act, our profession has been relatively silent about how we can approach testing constructively and effectively when it becomes mandatory. How can teachers negotiate the realities of a testing system without foregoing their classroom goals and pedagogical ideals? How can they help students do well on these tests while not revising their curricula to simply "teach to the test"? Although we are concerned about the burgeoning testing culture in education, we dedicate this short discussion to ways teachers can effectively approach these tests in their classrooms.

Preparation for standardized testing can be a difficult concept. How much do we sacrifice our normal goals in order to help students do well? How effective are such cramming methods, anyway? On the other hand, what will be the political fallout for our classrooms, our schools, and even our jobs if we are perceived as ignoring our responsibilities to the tests and the stakeholders who mandate them? Many of these tests are, at best, flawed. But the tests are a reality for many teachers—a reality that affects their professional status, the futures of their students, and their school's "grade" within a state accountability system. Like other issues we present in this book, there is no one right way to address standardized tests in the English classroom. Instead, we offer the following suggestions to guide teachers of English language arts.

Suggestions for Approaching High-Stakes Testing in English Language Arts Classes

Understand the test: Standardized tests differ from state to state (and often, depending on whims of state boards of education and legislatures, from year to year). It is important that English language arts teachers learn the format of the tests, how they are administered, and what types of activities or questions they include. Teachers need to understand the tests in order to inform their classroom practice.

Understand the standards on which tests are based: Many times we find that the standards each state recommends and that tests measure are theoretically and pedagogically sound. These are often devised, at least in part, by well-meaning English teachers and other educators and are consistent with the characteristics of effective English language arts classrooms. The Michigan English language arts standards, for example, include the following as their central motto:

> English language arts are the vehicles of communication by which we live, work, share, and build ideas and understandings of the present, reflect on the past, and imagine the future. Through the English language arts, we learn to appreciate, integrate, and apply what is learned for real purposes in our homes, schools, communities, and workplaces. (www. michigan.gov/mde/1,1607,7-140-6525_6530_6568-21282—,00.html)

While these standards are, for various reasons, often absent from or misconstrued on tests, knowledge of them will help an English language arts teacher justify his or her practices.

Consider how your class already prepares students for the test or meets the standards: Susan Tchudi and Stephen Tchudi (1999) remind us that "any decent reading and writing program—in particular one that has students read and write often—will naturally cover a great deal of what appears on any nationally-standardized test" (p. 62). We agree wholeheartedly; strong instruction that follows a teacher's inclination to get students reading, writing, and speaking can be the best preparation for any test.

Merge activities that prepare students for testing with existing assignments: The type of preparation is informed by knowing the implicit and explicit criteria, assumptions, characteristics, and methods of specific tests. Many testing skills and knowledge can be integrated within other projects without compromising the integrity of those projects. Many standardized writing tests, for example, use timed writing prompts, responses to texts, and other heuristics to facilitate student writing. These can be integrated into a larger writing project in which students write daily journals in response to prompts and then expand and develop these writings later. This activity can give students experience with timed prompts and help their test-taking skills while staying true to theories of composition instruction that emphasize process. Engaging students in discussions of various ways to respond to and develop these prompts can be even more valuable.

Do some test preparation: We make this suggestion hesitantly; we have both witnessed preparation weeks and other disruptive approaches to test preparation in which entire classes (or, in some cases, entire schools) stop regular instruction to focus on drills for upcoming state tests. We have even heard of schools having test pep rallies and other celebratory events! We believe that these sorts of activities are unnecessary and unproductive, placing too much emphasis on tests and creating unnecessary student and teacher stress.

Instead, we suggest that if a teacher feels comfortable doing so and it can be done in a way that doesn't disrupt the flow of a classroom curriculum or community, short activities simulating

the upcoming test or helping students analyze the potential audiences, purposes, and genres of the test (for writing assessments,
in particular) can enhance student knowledge and increase their
comfort level. We endorse activities that help students deconstruct
the context and audience for their writing (Who is going to be
reading this? What will be their evaluation rubric? What are some
appropriate ways to write for this prompt?), since such activities
may help students understand the testing context.

*Develop a standard rationale or philosophy for discussing your approach
to the tests:* Testing is a political phenomenon; the stances we take
toward tests are also political acts. Authors of the federal No Child
Left Behind Act advocate increased periodic testing of students
to ensure student learning and enforce teacher accountability. It
mandates annual testing for all students in grades 3 through 8 so
that "no child is left behind." Many political campaigns, whether
at the local, state, or national level, end up focusing to some extent on education, and often candidates equate student learning
and school improvement with increased testing. Such tests appear,
on the surface, to be a simple way to check up on schools. Many
educators, however, question the direct association of assessment
with learning and wonder if taking standardized tests could even
decrease learning when students spend more time during the
school year preparing for and taking exams than they do receiving instruction or engaging in learning activities. Whatever approach to these tests a teacher decides to take, he or she should
develop a philosophy to back up and justify those practices. Some
teachers take decidedly antitesting stances. It is the responsibility of these teachers to explain their principles and clearly, yet tact-
fully, communicate them to parents, fellow faculty, administrators, and other stakeholders. They should expect these views to
be controversial and should be prepared to defend and express
them professionally yet firmly.

Likewise, if a teacher takes an accommodationist view, in
which he or she accepts the tests and develops methods for integrating test preparation within current curricula, he or she can
also expect some colleagues to question this philosophy and practice. Therefore, we suggest that all teachers become well-versed
in testing issues and theories, as well as with the characteristics
of the specific tests required for their districts and states, in order
to develop and be able to articulate a philosophy supporting their
practice.

———

Narrative 3: Testing

The story told here is about a teacher's success with standardized testing. The teacher isn't deflated by widespread initial student failure but is instead determined to help her students pass the test. This narrative is from a high school in New York State.

The Retest Is Coming: What Should I Do?

When the New York State Board of Regents imposed mandatory passage of the newly designed English language arts Regents test for all students, a wave of panic reverberated through the classrooms. "How can this possibly be accomplished?" my colleagues gasped.

My response: carefully and systematically.

They eyed me with disbelief.

I began the year on day two by administering an entire ELA (English language arts) exam to incoming juniors. The frustration by the end of the week was as tangible as concrete. Eyes glazed, hands cramped, and eyelids drooped.

After grading four hundred essays in record time, my eyes glazed, hands cramped, and eyelids drooped, too. But what data spilled forth!

As I secretly anticipated, scores were dismal. Not a single student passed the exam. When I returned the tests, students stared in disbelief at the less than stellar scores. I then outlined a careful, systematic plan to improve scores to the deflated students in an attempt to ease their anxiety. Having had success preparing for previous exams and having spent countless hours locating resources and creating parallel tasks for every unit to be taught, I assured them that we were ready for the challenge. At least I was!

September to January was filled with deconstructing all of the tasks. Each week brought another piece of the writing puzzle to the forefront of instruction. Introductions fattened. Analyses deepened. Sentence structure varied. Thesis statements developed. Literary elements became their friends, and specific, accurate, and relevant data echoed as their mantra.

January's retest of the September exam rapidly approached. How would they fare this time?

Once again, they wrote the exam. This time seemed less labored, less frightening. They wondered: would their scores reflect all their efforts?

▶

Another four hundred essays later, we had our answer. Thesis statements, literary elements, and specific, accurate, and relevant data really are their friends. Eighty-nine of the one hundred students who would be required to take the Regents exam this year passed the test! And we still have five months to go. There's no stopping them now!

My mantra: carefully and systematically. That's how we need to approach all aspects of our English language arts curriculum.

A Teacher Responds

I'm torn in response to this case. I'm happy to hear about this teacher's successes, but I'm sad that she needed to spend so much time and effort preparing for a test.

Some positive things I think we can take from this: She clearly knows a lot about the exam her students were preparing to take. And I think this is an important lesson. When she first saw the dismal results of the initial exam, she isolated the things she knew would help students succeed on the next exam. Her phrase "carefully and systematically" captures this idea. She was not just grasping for concepts to focus on. Instead, she did her research and knew what her students needed to know, as her results show. I also like the fact that she talked briefly about parallel tasks, meaning that she was attempting to integrate test-specific skills within current projects. Additionally, the instruction she provides to students seems to be theoretically sound and appropriate, regardless of the testing situation.

My second response, though, is to be a bit worried. It's not clear how much this teacher changed her course to fit the needs of an exam that may have little real value for the development of her students' writing abilities. I'm concerned if we take from this narrative the lesson that we should completely change our classes in order to achieve higher test scores. More important, I'm wondering how her students felt about the changes in the class. Were they relieved that the class was going to help them pass a test that they feared? Were they upset that they didn't get the chance to do certain projects or writing activities that other classes had done in the past?

I don't have many answers for this case in terms of what the teacher should do. I do think she draws an excellent picture of the types of choices we make when confronted with an overwhelming test. Clearly, her students were discouraged by the test, and this teacher used her best judgment of their needs (both emotional and academic) to alleviate that discouragement. She did what she felt was right for the situation, and that decision was based on her understanding of the test, her school, and her students. Would I have done it differently? Probably. But I'm not sure either strategy is wrong.

For Further Discussion

1. The respondent believes there are many different ways to approach high-stakes testing. Working in a small group, consider the following question: If confronted with a situation like the one in the testing case (a group of discouraged, demoralized students who just failed a high-stakes test), what would be your initial plan? Why?

2. Consider some of the suggestions about test preparation provided in the previous narrative. What are the ones that appeal to you? Why?

Learning Activities

1. Look up your state's department of education (or equivalent) Web site. What is listed about standards and testing in English language arts? Is there information about a state test? Do they provide a sample test? Do you see disjunctions between the stated standards and the ways they are assessed?

2. In a small group, develop a means of assessing your school's (or a school with which you are familiar) effectiveness in English language arts that would be an alternative to a high-stakes test. Possibilities to consider include portfolios, writing-based assessments, local or "in-house" tests developed by individual teachers, etc.

Additional Resources about Standardized Testing

English Journal, 91(1), September 2001 issue.

> This themed issue of *English Journal* is a solid introduction to the thinking processes of teachers as they begin to address the complexities of teaching in an era of high-stakes testing.

FairTest: The National Center for Fair & Open Testing
www.fairtest.org

> FairTest is the best organized and most recognized of the test reform organizations currently active. Their Web site offers strong materials for teachers, parents, administrators, and others. Another organizational Web site (http://nochildleft.org) offers specific critique of the No Child Left Behind legislation driving current plans for national testing in reading.

Kohn, Alfie. (2000). *The Case against Standardized Testing: Raising the Scores, Ruining the Schools,* Portsmouth, NH: Heinemann.

> Kohn is an outspoken opponent of standardized testing. His text gives a strong overview of the testing culture, summarizes the goals of the standards movement, and advocates active resistance to both. He also provides alternative suggestions for assessing students.

National Council of Teachers of English and International Reading Association. (1996). *Standards for the English Language Arts.* Urbana, IL: NCTE and Newark, DE: IRA.

> This book provides the twelve content standards for K–12 developed by NCTE and IRA committees and then explains these standards and their classroom applications in detail. English teachers should be familiar with these standards and how they intersect with their state standards documents. The standards are also available electronically at www.ncte.org/standards/.

Ohanian, Susan. (1999). *One Size Fits Few: The Folly of Educational Standards.* Portsmouth, NH: Heinemann.

> Like Kohn, Ohanian is an outspoken opponent of standardized testing and the current standards culture in education. Drawing from her experiences as an educator, Ohanian critiques standards as dehumanizing and classist.

Your State Department of Education Web site or published state testing and standards materials.

> These materials are an invaluable resource for all English language arts teachers seeking to understand the intricacies of their state's standardized tests. A close examination of the assumptions and methods of these tests will assist teachers in developing their practices and philosophies.

In Closing

In a conversation with a veteran teacher, the following was said about a recent English education graduate: "She's so good with the kids, but she just does not know how to be collegial." Implicit in this statement and in the rest of the conversation is that teaching is much more than a curricular undertaking—it is a way of life that necessitates certain behaviors, such as collegiality with peers. Being a teacher is more than creating lesson plans, interacting with students, and dealing with objectives, grading, and other classroom activities. To be a teacher of English is to be a part of a local, regional, and national community. This particular new teacher was doing well in the aspects of teaching we often assess in teacher education programs: lesson planning, book selection, classroom management, assessment, etc. But instead of embracing her community and developing collegial, professional relationships with fellow teachers and administrators, she was retreating into her classroom, closing the doors, and developing an isolated teaching existence. We also hear from experienced teachers who feel disconnected from their field and alone in their classrooms. These teachers often end up leaving the profession because they feel lonely and unsupported.

We want to make it clear that we aren't blaming or chastising teachers who struggle with joining the teacher community and developing a professional identity. Becoming a teacher and being a teacher are difficult; the development of a professional identity often necessitates what feels like the giving up of a personal identity in favor of a culturally scripted "teacher" role. There are ways, however, of integrating personal beliefs and priorities with professional expectations, and over time there are even ways to change cultural definitions of what is an acceptable identity for the teacher. Teachers should not feel as though they have to give up their personal identities in order to teach. They may have to integrate these personal ideologies and subjectivities with professional responsibilities so that the two are not contradictory or working at cross-purposes, but such integration is possible, and when it occurs, a satisfying professional identity and a personal understanding of effective pedagogy results. Consider the following quote from Leila Christenbury (2000), a nationally recognized teacher and teacher educator:

> [A]fter my first fairly isolated semester, I began to seek—and find—other sources of help; I talked with other teachers, took courses, and began reading professional journals and books. Fellow and sister teachers gave advice and shared techniques; organizations such as the National Council of Teachers of English (NCTE) and my own state teaching organization published journals and held conferences. I tried to catch up as quickly as I could and become a teaching professional. (p. 3)

Christenbury (2000) describes her reliance as a new teacher on the local, regional, and national resources around her. Too many teachers close their doors and resort to working alone because of a fear of exposing weakness, a lack of confidence, or a school culture that encourages such isolation. We urge new teachers to instead seek out colleagues and mentors they can trust, share ideas and ask questions, join and be active in professional organizations, and, as much as possible, learn about the culture of a school before accepting a teaching job. We encourage more experienced teachers to engage in critical reflection of their practice, interact with colleagues, and mentor younger teachers. The best plan of action for reacting to unexpected and challenging situations in classrooms, be they related to classroom management, discipline, technology, testing, or anything else, is to use and seek out available resources and not get caught in the fallacy that to ask for help is to show weakness. The following suggested professional networks can provide knowledge and support for the new and the practicing teacher. We stress the importance of becoming an active part of a local, regional, and national teaching culture by

- forming a local study group about professional issues or problems. Such a group might read and discuss professional books or discuss various topics of importance;
- conducting teacher research with a team (see the conclusion for more specific ideas about teacher research) or informally talking with colleagues about classroom issues on a regular basis. Middle school teachers often work in teams, so they have a built-in network of peers; high school teachers might need to form their own networks;
- becoming active in the community's National Writing Project (NWP) site and participating in summer institutes, workshops, and other NWP professional development opportunities;
- taking a leadership position on local curriculum committees and with inservice initiatives and programs offered in local communities and school districts;
- becoming active in regional and national communities of English language arts teachers by joining the local NCTE affiliate (see www.ncte.org/affiliates for a complete list), keeping an active NCTE membership, and interacting in online NCTE initiatives such as the various listservs, CoLEARN (a new research and inquiry network developed by NCTE), and others.

The stories in this chapter narrate issues and concerns that are present in English teaching, even if sometimes we wish they would disappear. It's not as much fun to talk about classroom management and discipline, for example, as it is to discuss teaching a young adult novel. But these issues are real and must be considered carefully by the successful English teacher.

Conclusion: Narratives from *Your* Classroom— Using Stories to Facilitate Reflective Practice

Now that you have read and reflected on the stories throughout this book narrating the teaching of various aspects of English language arts in the secondary school, you might be wondering how you, a practicing or preservice English teacher, can use this information to improve your pedagogy. We believe that narrative is a valuable concept not only when it provides insight into the experiences of others from which we can learn vicariously but also when we are able to craft our own experiences as stories and then use this narrative structure as a heuristic or tool for critically deconstructing and understanding our experience.

This chapter explains how to understand events in your own classroom as stories that you can use as data from which to make new knowledge and improve the effectiveness of your classroom teaching. In order to describe this creation of narrative knowledge, we begin by defining some terms, namely *narratology, narrative research,* and *action research.* Then we describe how classroom teachers might conduct narrative action research in their classrooms to improve their practice and eventually their overall satisfaction with their professional lives. Many well-known teacher researchers have used narrative to structure, understand, and describe their pedagogical knowledge building (Tompkins, 1997; Rose, 1989, 1995; and Nancie Atwell, 1998); now it's your turn to do the same.

Narratology and Narrative Research

Narratology refers to narrative as an epistemology that sees story as central to the human experience and how human beings understand their worlds. Many of the early understandings about narrativity (such as Bruner's (1986) distinction of "paradigmatic" [i.e., logical] and "narrative" [i.e., conceptual] knowing and William Labov's schema for the trajectory of cohesive narratives [Labov & Waletzky, 1967]) emphasized linearity in form and singularity of purpose as important to a well-formed narrative. More contemporary narratologists, such as feminist researchers in the fields of education, psychology, anthropology, and the humanities, have rethought the ways in which narratives are structured and analyzed, often seeing stories as many-faceted rather than focused on a single purpose. Leslie Bloom (1998), for example, asserts that women's narratives will not follow a "traditional" structure moving from exposition, through climax, and on to a more or less neat resolution that usually puts the narrator in the role of hero or victor. Instead, they will contain several narrative threads that are sometimes contradictory but that represent the life of the narrator as multifaceted and complex. Bloom hypothesizes that such narratives represent what she calls the "nonunitary" subjectivities, or the various and often competing roles such subjectivities (or identities) play in the lives of woman who must, for example, regularly balance the competing demands of family and career. Stanton Wortham (2001) asserts that men's stories (and lives) also follow such complicated and nonlinear trajectories.

Narrative research refers both to this epistemology (seeing knowledge as narratively based) and to a more specific method for collecting and analyzing data—for example, asking research participants to narrate (usually autobiographical) stories about their experiences, which are then analyzed using a variety of discourse analysis tools or heuristics. D. Jean Clandinin and F. Michael Connelly (2000) define narrative research (sometimes called narrative inquiry) as "a way of understanding experience . . . in the midst of living and telling, reliving and retelling, the stories of the experiences that make up people's lives, both individual and social" (p. 20).

Narrative research has been undertaken in various disciplines, including anthropology, psychology, sociology, and education, and seems particularly well suited to qualitative or ethnographic studies of individuals within these disciplines, since, as Jerome Bruner (1986, 2002) asserted, people are essentially storytellers by nature. Bruner was among the first to advocate that personal narratives, in both content and form, actually *are* people's identities, not simply reflections of these identities. In other words, our identities are, in part, what we narrate to ourselves and to others, and through such narration (and its subsequent analysis) we can heighten our self-awareness and even make changes in the material reality of our worlds.

Teacher Action Research

Action research can be defined as research that grows from and leads to actual, practical (and often political and socially relevant) *actions*. Consequently, the term is often used when teacher research is being discussed, because teachers conducting research do so primarily for the purpose of learning what pedagogical actions to take to improve their teaching and their students' learning. Action research is also called teacher research, teacher inquiry, or practitioner research by various researchers and educators. While there are minor variations in how these terms are defined, in general they refer to similar processes of teachers systematically seeking knowledge in their classrooms. Cochran-Smith and Lytle (1993) define teacher research as "systematic and intentional inquiry by teachers about their own school and classroom work" (p. 23). Action research has been defined as "the study of a social situation with a view to improving the quality of action within it. . . . In action research, 'theories' are not validated independently and then applied to practice. They are validated through practice" (Elliott, 1991, p. 69).

All practitioner research has several characteristics in common: it is conducted by the "insider" or the teacher instead of an outside "researcher"; it uses qualitative or ethnographic methods such as interviewing, observation, "thick" description, or creation of case studies; and its goal is the improvement of classroom practice and the solving of professional problems through systematic and ongoing observation and analysis.

We believe that the concepts of narrative research and action research are quite compatible. While narrative research does not automatically imply a researcher as practitioner conducting research in his or her own classroom, the creation and analysis of experience as story is a powerful way of conducting teacher action research. Clandinin and Connelly (2000) list several characteristics of narrative inquiry that seem particularly applicable to teacher action research and that emphasize the usefulness to teachers of conducting classroom narrative analysis:

1. *Temporality:* Clandinin and Connelly see temporality as central to narrative research: "Any event, or thing, has a past, a present as it appears to us, and an implied future" (p. 29). In other words, decisions that are made about education, ranging from classroom-specific pedagogical decisions to school- or districtwide curricular decisions, are made in the context of what has been done in the past, what might be happening now with students or in the school, and the goals for the future. Narratives tell the story of an event that occurs in a certain

space and time; hence, longitudinal or long-term analysis of such narratives could certainly help a teacher learn about the effectiveness of his teaching and make plans to improve it if necessary.

2. *People:* Narrative research assumes the existence of human beings in the stories that are told, listened to, and analyzed. Clandinin and Connelly suggest that the narrative histories of students be taken into account as pedagogical and curricular decisions are made. They write, "We take for granted that people, at any point in time, are in a process of personal change and that from an educational point of view, it is important to be able to narrate the person in terms of the process" (p. 30). Action research takes an ethnographic stance that requires observation of and interaction with people (i.e., students) in the research setting.

3. *Action:* In narrative research, actions are viewed as being a result of narrative histories or autobiographical (personal or professional) experiences. In other words, the teacher makes the pedagogical decisions she does because of her past teaching life and how she understands it. Teacher action research is also about material actions or enactments of teachers and students in a particular classroom context—about both understanding those that are currently occurring and making informed decisions about what actions to undertake in the future.

4. *Certainty:* In narrative research, as in action research, interpretations of narrative data vary depending on the context, the expectations of the researcher, and the research questions or goals. There is a "sense of tentativeness" (p. 31) about the "meaning" of stories as research texts. Certainty of "results" is replaced by a search for the trustworthiness and usefulness of results in improving practice.

5. *Context:* Clandinin and Connelly state, "In narrative thinking, context is ever present. It includes such notions as temporal context, spatial context, and context of other people" (p. 32). It is vital in both narrative research and action research to pay close attention to the context of a research project in order to make sense of data and create new knowledge.

What Does This Mean for You? Using Narrative Action Research to Improve Classroom Practice

What follows are some general suggestions for conducting narrative action research in your classroom. These suggestions are guidelines you can use as a beginning researcher learning to understand your teaching and improve it through stories. At the end of this section, we discuss some specific ways to analyze narratives from your classroom in order to make sense of them and tap them for pedagogical knowledge. In its essence, we see the entire process as one of inquiry and subsequent knowledge building, with stories as the core. The reflective practitioner is one who not only asks questions about his or her practice and observes the events in his or her classroom but also forms hypotheses about how to modify practices that lead to actual change and improvement over time. One way to begin this process of observation and informed decision making is by becoming a teacher researcher.

1. Deciding on a Research Question(s). The first thing you need to do is think about what aspects of your classroom concern or intrigue you. What would you like to know about your classroom teaching and your students' learning? These research questions will probably start broad (e.g., why don't my students like to read?) and get narrower with time and consideration (e.g., what genres have more appeal to my male students?). At these first stages of the research process, you might consider keeping a teaching journal or jotting down questions that come to you during the teaching day. Give yourself time to explore and reflect before deciding on a question. What do you want to know? What bothers you? What do you think about when you are lying in bed at night mentally planning the next day? These writings can be revisited at the end of a school day or week to help you craft a research question that is complex enough to be meaningful yet focused enough to be adequately addressed through classroom research. Remember that once you become a classroom researcher, you will always be one, so you will have plenty of time to explore all of your pedagogical questions!

2. Strategies for Narrative Data Collection. Next, start keeping a "story log" of events that you see going on in your classroom. You might be able to jot down some stories (or brief notes to remind you of stories) during the school day, or if time does not allow for this, set aside fifteen to twenty minutes at the end of the school day to write. These narratives should be as focused as possible around your research question. If, for example, your question is about what genres of literature boys in your classroom tend to prefer reading, you might make note of a conversation you had with a male student during free reading time or a scene you witnessed in which two male students browsed the library and discussed what they like to read. Another way to gather research narratives is to ask students to tell you stories about their literacy learning histories and/or experiences or to write autobiographies of themselves as readers and writers. For the purposes of your research, you might think of the narratives, both written and oral, you collect from yourself and your students as having the following characteristics: (1) a chronological structure telling of an event or events that are habitual, that occurred in the past, are occurring in the present, or will occur in the future; (2) a beginning, a middle, and an end, however loosely defined; (3) a setting or context; and (4) either an explicit explanation of meaning or an implied meaning or purpose for the story. We also recommend keeping artifacts related to your research, such as assignments students have completed. These artifacts, while not narratives in their own right, will become part of a student's story as you begin to analyze all of your data.

Additionally, you might think about an organizational structure for keeping the narratives you collect. You might, for example, keep a series of folders in which you file stories written or told by individual students in separate files. You might consider focusing on a single student or only a few students so as not to get overwhelmed with data. If your research question began as "Why can't I get students to work productively in peer writing groups?," for example, you might decide to focus on one group that seems particularly problematic or unproductive. These students may be asked to engage in short interviews or conversations with you (that you might audiotape or take notes about immediately afterward) in which you ask them to tell you a story about the last time the group met. Then you can watch them work as a group and take your own narrative notes about their process. You might also collect artifacts such as the students' papers as they appeared both before and after the peer review process.

3. Analysis of the Narratives. Now that you have collected many narratives and associated artifacts, how do you make sense of what you have? Data analysis, which is in many ways ongoing during the entire data collection process, begins in earnest when the data have been collected. Here are some ways you can analyze or understand the stories from your classroom. Usually, a researcher uses more than one of these approaches when looking at a single data set:

- *Conceptual Analysis:* In conceptual analysis, you read through your narratives and associated relevant artifacts and allow thematic categories to emerge. In other words, you read your stories several times, perhaps taking notes in the margins when interesting ideas or concepts appear or highlighting areas of interest. You will begin to notice that similar ideas, interesting issues, or student comments and actions begin to reappear. This repetition or reappearance is possible evidence of something important going on in your classroom and should be noted. You should "name" the issue, concept, or action that reappears, and then it becomes a "category" or "code." Such categories or codes are expanded or collapsed as the data continue to be reread, and they eventually become statements of importance or preliminary theories or findings of the research.

- *Formal Analysis:* When conducting this type of analysis, you look at formal features of the language—e.g., word choice, use of imagery such as metaphor, how questions are asked and answered, how praise is given or received, length of student responses, complexity of oral or written sentences, etc. This type of analysis can be used in collaboration with conceptual analysis to provide deeper understandings of the data, particularly for the English teacher, who is often concerned with the changes students undergo in the quality and complexity of language use.
- *Comparative Analysis:* Comparative analysis compares the above characteristics across students, across time, or across contexts and notes any trends.

4. Enacting Classroom Change. This is the last, and an important, step. Now that you have collected and analyzed narrative data, so what? What did you learn from your narratives and their analysis? How can what you learned lead to classroom change and improvement in your teaching? Just as you have used the narratives in this book as windows into secondary English teaching and as prompts for discussion of pedagogical strategies and theoretical perspectives, you will be able to critically reflect on your own narratives and explore ways to improve the quality of your teaching and increase student learning in the classes you teach. Constructing classroom experiences as narratives provides a way to make your classroom practices explicit so that you can reflect on them and their consistency with your overall teaching beliefs and philosophy.

Ethical Issues in Narrative Action Research

We think it is important to include a few words about ethical issues that should be considered and recognized when conducting action research. First, pseudonyms should be used to refer to all students, parents, or other individuals who are referred to or described in your research, especially when this research is distributed to or shared with an audience.

Many aspects of a student's classroom experiences (i.e., grades they receive, disciplinary referrals, parent conferences about them, etc.) should remain confidential because of possible embarrassment or harm that could result for the student, parent, or other individual mentioned and also to be in compliance with laws mandating confidentiality of student records. Second, students and parents should be in the loop about your project as much as is possible or feasible, and research participants should give full, written permission if you intend to share your research in the form of conference presentations, articles in teaching journals or books, or at inservice workshops. It is a good idea to check with your school district or corporation to see it has a policy or procedures in place for teachers conducting classroom research; a district, for example, might have its own set of permission forms that should be signed by participants prior to the beginning of a research project. Last, it is important to reflect on your assumptions about the research context before beginning data collection and to consider your biases and/or expectations for what the research will demonstrate. Being aware of these assumptions, expectations, and biases will help you remain open to the ideas that the project reveals to you instead of unconsciously directing the project toward certain results or prematurely closing off the possibility of unexpected insights.

Additional Resources to Consult about Narrative Teacher Research

Hubbard, Ruth Shagoury, and Brenda Miller Power. (1993). *The Art of Classroom Inquiry: A Handbook for Teacher-Researchers.* Portsmouth, NH: Heinemann.

> This book is a practical guide for conducting teacher research. It gives step-by-step instructions for how to collect and analyze data and for sharing research results with a wider audience.

Jalongo, Mary Renck, and Joan P. Isenberg, with Gloria Gerbracht. (1995). *Teachers' Stories: From Personal Narrative to Professional Insight.* San Francisco: Jossey-Bass.

> Jalongo and Isenberg describe how teachers' stories can become more than just personal representations of experience; they can be ways to critically reflect on practice. They include examples of strategies to encourage the telling of stories and how to go about using these stories for professional development.

Lieblich, Amia, Rivka Tuval-Mashiach, and Tamar Zilber. (1998). *Narrative Research: Reading, Analysis and Interpretation.* Thousand Oaks, CA: Sage.

This book provides detailed descriptions of how to engage in different kinds of narrative analysis, including holistic analysis and categorical analysis.

Seidman, Irving. (1998). *Interviewing as Qualitative Research: A Guide for Researchers in Education and the Social Sciences* (2nd ed.). New York: Teachers College Press.

This book describes in detail the process of interviewing, explaining how best to go about interviewing research participants to gather meaningful data without dominating conversations or violating participants' privacy. Interviewing is viewed as a relationship between the researcher and participant.

Zeni, Jane (Ed.). (2001). *Ethical Issues in Practitioner Research.* New York: Teachers College Press.

This collection of essays explores such issues as why we engage in teacher research, who benefits from it, and who "owns" the results.

References

Allen, J. (1995). *It's never too late: Leading adolescents to lifelong literacy*. Portsmouth, NH: Heinemann.

Alvermann, D. E., Moon, J. S., & Hagood, M. C. (1999). *Popular culture in the classroom: Teaching and researching critical media literacy*. Newark, DE: International Reading Association.

Ammon, P. (1985). Helping children learn to write in ESL: Some observations and hypotheses. In S. W. Freedman (Ed.), *The acquisition of written language: Response and revision* (pp. 65–84). Norwood, NJ: Ablex.

Anderson, P. M., & Rubano, G. (1991). *Enhancing aesthetic reading and response*. Urbana, IL: National Council of Teachers of English.

Armbruster, K., & Wallace, K. R. (Eds.). (2001). *Beyond nature writing: Expanding the boundaries of ecocriticism*. Charlottesville: University Press of Virginia.

Arnheim, R. (1969). *Visual thinking*. Berkeley: University of California Press.

Asimov, N. (1998, June 3). Big victory for measure to end bilingual education: Opponents say they'll file suit today. *San Francisco Chronicle*, p. 31. Retrieved August 18, 2003, from http://sfgate.com/.

Assembly for the Teaching of English Grammar (ATEG). (n.d.). Some questions and answers about grammar (NCTE Positions and Guidelines). Retrieved August 4, 2003, from http://www.ncte.org/positions/grammar.shtml.

Atwell, N. (1998). *In the middle: New understandings about writing, reading, and learning*. Portsmouth, NH: Boynton/Cook.

Azar, B. S. (2002). *Understanding and using English grammar* (3rd ed.). White Plains, NY: Pearson Education.

Baker, C. (1996). *Foundations of bilingual education and bilingualism* (2nd ed.). Clevedon, England: Multilingual Matters.

Bartolome, L. I. (1994). Beyond the methods fetish: Toward a humanizing pedagogy. *Harvard Educational Review, 64*(2), 173–94.

Berlin, J. A. (1988). Rhetoric and ideology in the writing class, *College English, 50*(5), 477–94.

Berlin, J. A. (1996). *Rhetorics, poetics, and cultures: Refiguring college English studies*. Urbana, IL: National Council of Teachers of English.

Berman, P., Chambers, J., Gandara, P., McLaughlin, B., Minicucci, C., Nelson, B., Olsen, L., & Parrish, T. (1992). *Meeting the challenge of language diversity: An evaluation of programs for pupils with limited proficiency in English*. Berkeley, CA: BW Associates.

Bizzell, P. (1992). *Academic discourse and critical consciousness.* Pittsburgh: University of Pittsburgh Press.

Bloom, L. R. (1998). *Under the sign of hope: Feminist methodology and narrative interpretation.* Albany: State University of New York Press.

Bracey, G. W. (2003). *What you should know about the war against America's public schools.* Boston: Allyn and Bacon.

Braddock, R. R., Lloyd-Jones, R., & Schoer, L. A. (1963). *Research in written composition.* Urbana, IL: National Council of Teachers of English.

Britton, J. N. (1975). *The development of writing abilities (11–18).* London: Macmillan.

Britzman, D. P. (1991). *Practice makes practice: A critical study of learning to teach.* Albany: State University of New York Press.

Bruner, J. (1986). *Actual minds, possible worlds.* Cambridge, MA: Harvard University Press.

Bruner, J. S. (2002). *Making stories: Law, literature, life.* New York: Farrar, Straus & Giroux.

Carey-Webb, A. (2001). *Literature and lives: A response-based, cultural studies approach to teaching English.* Urbana, IL: National Council of Teachers of English.

Carter, K. (1993). The place of story in the study of teaching and teacher education. *Educational Researcher, 22* (January–February), 5–8.

Chamot, A. U., & O'Malley, J. M. (1994). *The CALLA handbook: Implementing the cognitive academic language learning approach.* Reading, MA: Addison-Wesley.

Chappel, J. M. (1998). Literature circles in intermediate science. In S. Zemelman, H. Daniels, & A. A. Hyde, *Best practice: New standards for teaching and learning in America's schools* (pp. 125–31). Portsmouth, NH: Heinemann.

Chomsky, N. (1957). *Syntactic structures.* The Hague, Netherlands: Mouton.

Christenbury, L. (2000). *Making the journey: Being and becoming a teacher of English language arts* (2nd ed.). Portsmouth, NH: Boynton/Cook.

Churchward, B. (2003). *Discipline by design: The honor level system.* Retrieved August 5, 2003, from http://www.honorlevel.com.

Clandinin, D. J., & F. M. Connelly. (2000). *Narrative inquiry: Experience and story in qualitative research.* San Francisco: Jossey-Bass.

Cochran-Smith, M., & Lytle, S. L. (1993). *Inside/outside: Teacher research and knowledge.* New York: Teachers College Press.

Collier, V. P. (1995). Acquiring a second language for school. *Directions in Language and Education, 1*(4), 1–12.

Conference on College Composition and Communication (CCCC). (1974). Students' right to their own language (CCCC Position Statements). Retrieved August 1, 2003, from http://www.ncte.org/cccc/positions/right_to_language.shtml.

Daniels, H. (1994). *Literature circles: Voice and choice in the student-centered classroom.* Portland, ME: Stenhouse.

Daniels, H. (2002). *Literature circles: Voice and choice in book clubs and reading groups.* Portland, ME: Stenhouse.

Daniels, H., & Bizar, M. (1998). *Methods that matter: Six structures for best practice classrooms.* Portland, ME: Stenhouse.

Dewey, J. (1938). *Experience and education.* New York: Collier Books.

Diaz-Rico, L. T., & Weed, K. Z. (1995). *The crosscultural, language, and academic development handbook.* Boston: Allyn and Bacon.

Donelson, K. L., & Nilsen, A. P. (1997). *Literature for today's young adults* (5th ed.). New York: Longman.

Doniger, P. E. (2003). Language matters: Grammar as a tool in the teaching of literature. *English Journal, 92,* 101–04.

Echevarria, J., Vogt, M. E., & Short, D. J. (2000). *Making content comprehensible for English language learners: The SIOP model.* Boston: Allyn and Bacon.

Edelsky, C. (1981). From "JIMOSALCO" to "7 naranjas se calleron e el arbolest-triste en lagrymas": Writing development in a bilingual program. In B. Cronnell (Ed.), *The writing needs of linguistically different students: The proceedings of a research/practice conference held at SWRL Educational Research and Development, Los Alamitos, Calif., June 25–26, 1981* (pp. 63–98). Los Alamitos, CA: Southwest Regional Laboratory.

Edelsky, C. (1982). *Development of writing in a bilingual program* (Final Report, Grant No. NIE-G-81-0051, National Institute of Education). Tempe: Arizona State University.

Elbow, P. (1973). *Writing without teachers.* New York: Oxford University Press.

Elliott, J. (1991). *Action research for educational change.* Milton Keynes, England: Open University Press.

Emig, J. A. (1971). *The composing processes of twelfth graders.* Urbana, IL: National Council of Teachers of English.

Faltis, C. J., & Hudelson, S. J. (1998). *Bilingual education in elementary and secondary school communities: Toward understanding and caring.* Boston: Allyn and Bacon.

Fox, R. F. (1994). *Images in language, media, and mind.* Urbana, IL: National Council of Teachers of English.

Fulwiler, T. (1987). *The journal book.* Portsmouth, NH: Boynton/Cook.

Fulwiler, T., & Young, A. (Eds.). (1990). *Programs that work: Models and methods for Writing Across the Curriculum.* Portsmouth, NH: Boynton/Cook.

Gardner, H. (1983). *Frames of mind: The theory of multiple intelligences.* New York: Basic Books.

Glotfelty, C., & Fromm, H. (Eds.). (1996). *The Ecocriticism Reader: Landmarks in Literary Ecology.* Athens, University of Georgia Press.

Gonzalez, R. D. (1990). When minority becomes majority: The changing face of English classrooms. *English Journal, 79*(1), 16–23.

Goodman, K. S., Bird, L. B., & Goodman, Y. M. (1991). *The whole language catalog*. Santa Rosa, CA: American School Publishers.

Goodman, K. S., & Goodman, Y. M. (1978). Reading of American children whose language is a stable rural dialect of English or a language other than English. Final Report, Project NIE-C-003-0087. Washington, DC: National Institute of Education.

Goodman, K. S., Goodman, Y. M., & Hood, W. J. (Eds.). (1989). *The whole language evaluation book*. Portsmouth, NH: Heinemann.

Goodman, Y. M. (1996). *Notes from a kidwatcher: Selected writings of Yetta M. Goodman*. S. Wilde (Ed.). Portsmouth, NH: Heinemann.

Goodman, Y. M., & Wilde, S. (Eds.). (1992). *Literacy events in a community of young writers*. New York: Teachers College Press.

Halliday, M. A. K. (1994). The place of dialogue in children's construction of meaning. In R. B. Ruddell, M. R. Ruddell, & H. Singer (Eds.), *Theoretical models and processes of reading* (4th ed.). Newark, DE: International Reading Association.

Haswell, R. H. (1983). Minimal marking. *College English, 45,* 600–604.

Hernandez-Chavez, E. (1984). The inadequacy of English immersion education as an educational approach for language minority students in the United States. In Office of Bilingual Bicultural Education, *Studies in immersion education: A collection for United States educators* (pp.144–83). Sacramento: California State Department of Education.

Herz, S. K., & Gallo, D. R. (1996). *From Hinton to Hamlet: Building bridges between young adult literature and the classics*. Westport, CT: Greenwood Press.

Holt, J. R. (1982). In defense of formal grammar. *Curriculum Review, 21,* 173–78.

Hudelson, S. (Ed.). (1981). *Learning to read in different languages*. Washington, DC: Center for Applied Linguistics.

Hunt, K. W. (1966). Recent measures in syntactic development. *Elementary English, 43,* 732–39.

Hunt, K. W. (1970). *Syntactic maturity in schoolchildren and adults*. Monographs of the Society for Research in Child Development, No. 134. Chicago: University of Chicago Press.

Hunt, K. W. (1977). Early blooming and late blooming syntactic structures. In C. R. Cooper & L. Odell (Eds.), *Evaluating writing: Describing, measuring, judging* (pp. 94–104). Urbana, IL: National Council of Teachers of English.

Johnston, P. H., & Allington, R. L. (2002). *Reading to learn: Lessons from exemplary fourth-grade classrooms*. New York: Guilford Press.

Kaywell, J. F. (Ed.). (1993). *Adolescent literature as a complement to the classics* (Vols. 1–4). Norwood, MA: Christopher-Gordon.

Kohn, A. (2000). *The case against standardized testing: Raising the scores, ruining the schools*. Portsmouth, NH: Heinemann.

Kolln, M. (1981). Closing the books on alchemy. *College Composition and Communication, 32,* 139–51.

Krashen, S. D. (1982). *Principles and practice in second language acquisition.* Oxford: Pergamon Press.

Labov, W., & Waletzky, J. (1967). Narrative analysis: Oral versions of personal experience. In J. Helm (Ed.). *Essays on the verbal and visual arts* (pp. 12–44). Seattle: University of Washington Press.

Larson, R. L. (1967). Teaching before we judge: Planning assignments in composition. *The Leaflet, 66*(1), 3–15.

Luke, C. (1997). Media literacy and cultural studies. In S. Muspratt, A. Luke, & P. Freebody (Eds.), *Constructing critical literacies* (pp. 19–50). Cresskill, NJ: Hampton Press.

Macrorie, K. (1976). *Writing to be read.* Rochelle Park, NJ: Hayden.

Macrorie, K. (1988). *The I-search paper.* Portsmouth, NH: Boynton/Cook.

Mazel, D. (2000). *American literary environmentalism.* Athens: University of Georgia Press.

McGroarty, M. (2002). Evolving influences on educational language policies. In J. W. Tollefson (Ed.), *Language policies in education: Critical issues* (pp. 17–36). Mahwah, NJ: Erlbaum.

Moffett, J. (1983). *Teaching the universe of discourse.* Portsmouth, NH: Boynton/Cook.

Moffett, J., & Wagner, B. J. (1992). *Student-centered language arts, K–12.* Portsmouth, NH: Boynton/Cook.

Monseau, V. R. (1996). *Responding to young adult literature.* Portsmouth, NH: Boynton/Cook.

Murray, D. (1982). *Learning by teaching: Selected articles on writing and teaching.* Montclair, NJ: Boynton/Cook.

Murray, D. (1985). *A writer teaches writing: A practical method of teaching composition.* Boston: Houghton Mifflin.

Myers, M., & Spalding, E. (Eds.). (1997). *Standards exemplar series: Assessing student performance: Grades 9–12.* Urbana, IL: National Council of Teachers of English.

National Commission on Excellence in Education. (1983). A nation at risk: The imperative for educational reform. Washington, DC: Author.

National Council of Teachers of English and International Reading Association. (1996). *Standards for the English language arts.* Urbana, IL, and Newark, DE: Authors.

Nelms, B. F. (1988). *Literature in the classroom: Readers, texts, and contexts.* Urbana, IL: National Council of Teachers of English.

Neuleib, J. (1977). The relation of formal grammar to composition. *College Composition and Communication, 28,* 247–50.

Newkirk, T. (1990). *To compose: Teaching writing in high school and college* (2nd ed.). Portsmouth, NH: Boynton/Cook.

Noden, H. R. (1999). *Image grammar: Using grammatical structures to teach writing.* Portsmouth, NH: Heinemann.

Ohanian, S. (1999). *One size fits few: The folly of educational standards.* Portsmouth, NH: Heinemann.

Ovando, C. J., & Collier, V. P. (1998). *Bilingual and ESL classrooms: Teaching in multicultural contexts* (2nd ed). Boston: McGraw-Hill.

Peregoy, S. F., & Boyle, O. F. (2001). *Reading, writing, and learning in ESL: A resource book for K–12 teachers* (3rd ed.). New York: Longman.

Phillips, D. C. (1995). The good, the bad, and the ugly: The many faces of constructivism. *Educational Researcher, 24*(7), 5–12.

Piaget, J. (1926). *The language and thought of the child.* New York: Harcourt, Brace, & World.

Probst, R. E. (1988). *Response and analysis: Teaching literature in junior and senior high school.* Portsmouth, NH: Boynton/Cook.

Purves, A., Rogers, T., & Soter, A. O. (1995). *How porcupines make love III: Readers, texts, cultures in the response-based literature classroom* (2nd ed.). White Plains, NY: Longman.

Ramirez, J. D. (1992). Executive summary of the final report. *Bilingual Research Journal, 16*, 1–62.

Ramirez, J. D., Yuen, S. D., Ramey, D. R., & Pasta, D. J. (1991). *Final report: Longitudinal study of structured English immersion strategy, early-exit and late-exit transitional bilingual education programs for language-minority children* (Vols. 1, 2). San Mateo, CA: Aguirre International.

Romano, T. (1987). *Clearing the way: Working with teenage writers.* Portsmouth, NH: Heinemann.

Romano, T. (2000). *Blending genre, altering style: Writing multigenre papers.* Portsmouth, NH: Boynton/Cook.

Rose, M. (1989). *Lives on the boundary: The struggles and achievements of America's underprepared.* New York: Free Press.

Rose, M. (1995). *Possible lives: The promise of public education in America.* Boston: Houghton Mifflin.

Rosenblatt, L. M. (1978). *The reader, the text, the poem: The transactional theory of the literary work.* Carbondale: Southern Illinois University Press.

Rosenblatt, L. M. (1982). The literary transaction: Evocation and response. *Theory into Practice, 21*(4), 268–77.

Rosenblatt, L. (1983). *Literature as exploration* (4th ed.). New York: Modern Language Association (Original work published 1938).

Sams, L. (2003). How to teach grammar, analytical thinking, and writing: A method that works. *English Journal, 92*(3), 57–65.

Schlechty, P. E. (2002). *Working on the work: An action plan for teachers, princi- pals, and superintendents*. San Francisco: Jossey-Bass.

Scholes, R. E. (1985). *Textual power: Literary theory and the teaching of English.* New Haven, CT: Yale University Press.

Schunk, D. H. (1991). *Learning theories: An educational perspective.* New York: Merrill.

Silva, T. (1993). Toward an understanding of the distinct nature of L2 writing: The ESL research and its implications. *TESOL Quarterly, 27*(4), 657–75.

Skinner, B. F. (1957). *Verbal behavior.* New York: Appleton-Century-Crofts.

Smith, F. (1978). *Understanding reading: A psycholinguistic analysis of reading and learning to read* (2nd ed.). New York: Holt, Rinehart and Winston.

Smith, F. (1988). *Joining the literacy club: Further essays into education.* Ports- mouth, NH: Heinemann.

Smith, M. W., & Wilhelm, J. D. (2002). *"Reading don't fix no Chevys": Literacy in the lives of young men.* Portsmouth, NH: Heinemann.

Snow, M. A. (2000). *Implementing the ESL standards for pre-K–12 students through teacher education.* Alexandria, VA: TESOL Publications.

Solzhenitsyn, A. (1998). *One day in the life of Ivan Denisovich.* New York: Signet Classic.

Sonntag, S. K., & Pool, J. (1987). Linguistic denial and linguistic self-denial: American ideologies of language. *Language Problems and Language Planning* 11, 46-65.

Tchudi, S. J., & Tchudi, S. N. (1999). *The English language arts handbook: Classroom strategies for teachers* (2nd ed.). Portsmouth, NH: Boynton/ Cook.

Teachers of English to Speakers of Other Languages (TESOL). (1997). *ESL standards for pre-K–12 students.* Alexandria, VA: Author.

Thomas W., & Collier, V. P. (1995). *Language minority student achievement and program effectiveness.* Washington, DC: National Clearinghouse for Bilingual Education.

Tollefson, J. W. (2002). *Language policies in education: Critical issues.* Mahwah, NJ: Erlbaum.

Tompkins, J. P. (1997). *A life in school: What the teacher learned.* Reading, MA: Addison-Wesley.

Trimbur, J. (1989). Consensus and difference in collaborative learning. *College English, 51*(6), 602–16.

Vygotsky, L. S. (1962). *Thought and language.* Cambridge, MA: M.I.T. Press.

Vygotsky, L. S. (1987). In R. W. Rieber & A. S. Carton (Eds.), *The collected works of L. S. Vygotsky.* New York: Plenum Press.

Walling, D. R. (1993). *English as a second language: 25 questions and answers.* Bloomington, IN: Phi Delta Kappa Educational Foundation.

Weaver, C. (1996). *Teaching grammar in context.* Portsmouth, NH: Boynton/ Cook.

Weaver, C. (Ed.). (1998). *Lessons to share on teaching grammar in context.* Portsmouth, NH: Boynton/Cook.

Wilhelm, J. (1995). *"You gotta BE the book": Teaching engaged and reflective reading with adolescents.* New York: Teachers College Press.

Wortham, S. E. F. (2001). *Narratives in action: A strategy for research and analysis.* New York: Teachers College Press.

Zemelman, S., Daniels, H., & Hyde, A. A. (1998). *Best practice: New standards for teaching and learning in America's schools.* Portsmouth, NH: Heinemann.

Index

Authors

Janet Alsup is assistant professor of English education at Purdue University, where she teaches undergraduate courses in the teaching of writing and literature in the secondary school and graduate courses in young adult literature and reading. She has published articles in *English Education; Pedagogy: Critical Approaches to Teaching Literature, Language, Composition, and Culture; The ALAN Review;* and the *Journal of Adolescent and Adult Literacy.* She presents regularly at the NCTE Annual Convention and the Conference on College Composition and Communication Annual Convention. Currently, she is working on a book about the professional identity development of preservice English teachers.

Jonathan Bush is assistant professor of English education at Western Michigan University, where he co-directs the Third Coast Writing Project. He teaches undergraduate courses in elementary and secondary English methods and graduate courses in composition theory and practice. He has published in *English Education, English Leadership Quarterly,* and *Contemporary Issues in Technology and Teacher Education* and is a regular presenter at the NCTE Annual Convention and the annual convention of the Conference on College Composition and Communication. He is also coeditor of the *Language Arts Journal of Michigan.*

This book was typeset in Palatino and Helvetica by Electronic Imaging.
Typefaces used on the cover were Bank Gothic and Helvetica Narrow Bold.
The book was printed on 50-lb. Husky Offset paper by IPC Printing Services.